Business Tools, Not Platitudes

Business Tools, Not Platitudes

*With Staff
Training Modules*

Lloyd Lim

ARCHWAY
PUBLISHING

Archway Publishing books may be ordered through booksellers or by contacting:

Archway Publishing
1663 Liberty Drive
Bloomington, IN 47403
www.archwaypublishing.com
1 (888) 242-5904

Because of the dynamic nature of the Internet, any web addresses or links contained in this book may have changed since publication and may no longer be valid. The views expressed in this work are solely those of the author and do not necessarily reflect the views of the publisher, and the publisher hereby disclaims any responsibility for them.

Any people depicted in stock imagery provided by Thinkstock are models, and such images are being used for illustrative purposes only. Certain stock imagery © Thinkstock.

ISBN: 978-1-4808-5003-3 (sc)
ISBN: 978-1-4808-5004-0 (e)

Library of Congress Control Number: 2017948988

Print information available on the last page.

Archway Publishing rev. date: 07/18/2017

Dedication

For my mother and father, who ran a small
mom-and-pop business, were devoted to their
children, and were a team in life and in work.

Contents

Acknowledgments

My business acquaintances Janis Akuna, Calvin Hutton, and Sam Thomsen reviewed an early draft of this book. My academic acquaintance Colin Moore checked my futurist projections in chapter 21. My college friend Harry Imster gave input on client management which can be found in chapter 3. I also discussed client management with my business acquaintances Jaymes Song and again Calvin Hutton. My CPA, Paul K. Green, gave input on some of the technical things people starting a business tend to miss which can be found in chapter 5. My childhood friend Christopher Campbell gave additional input that I added to chapter 7.

I also owe thanks to my business school professors and to many of my work colleagues and supervisors from whom I have learned things both good and bad. I particularly thank those who taught me the value of simplicity (following Ockham, Einstein, and the pianist Josef Hofmann)—my music teachers Dean Immel, Piero Weiss, and Niels Ostbye and one of my first lawyer-supervisors, Charles Sanders.

And of course, much gratitude to my parents, who made a decision not to shield me from the issues arising in our family business even when I was in my early teens.

Introduction

At one time, people went to beauty salons and spas to have mud put on their faces and cold cucumbers put on their eyes. It doesn't do anything, but it feels good. That, unfortunately, is what some business consulting is like today: many platitudes, goals, and generalities, but few specifics about how to actually get from point A to point B. As for me, I value my credibility far too much to engage in "snake oil" salesmanship. As for you, by buying this relatively inexpensive book, you are distinguishing yourself from a CEO who is merely trying to impress his or her board members by hiring the latest "guru" to blow smoke up everyone's you-know-what. If you are as tired as I am of wasting money on "nothing burger" business books, then you will appreciate the amount of value that I have packed into this relatively short text.

I am not trying to create business geniuses. I merely want to set a floor below which our businesspeople do not fall, particularly if they are first-time entrepreneurs. I want to sensitize them so that they can spot issues, ask the right questions, and learn for themselves. Teach a person to fish, as it were. This is the better approach because as the world changes, the answers to some of our questions will also. Indeed, there will even be some new questions.

Those of us who have tried to come up with new business ideas sometimes feel like the eccentric inventor Dr. Emmett Brown (played by Christopher Lloyd) in the *Back to the Future* movies. It is not uncommon to get laughed at. Entrepreneurs test dreams against the harsh reality of the market, and the experience can be humbling. But we learn as we go, and that is part of the fun. America was built on dreams, and without dreams, there can be no progress.

That said, you have to keep your feet on the ground to some extent. I know someone who had an idea for a device that required heavy IT programming, but she didn't have any background in computers. She wanted to hire someone to do the programming for her "invention," as she put it. I said: "if you don't do the programming, then it is not your invention." Unfortunately she didn't listen to me and ended up spending big money foolishly on the project. Similarly, when I first started writing twenty-five years ago, a publisher suggested that because I was a lawyer I should write fiction about lawyers like John Grisham. Good idea, except I'm not great at fiction writing, particularly in the long format. So while it is important to dream, you have to know yourself. Your business should grow out of your natural strengths.

This book is short because most people are busy and don't have time for nonsense. At bottom, business is simple, at least conceptually. The devil is in the details. The place where concept meets reality and the rubber meets the road is where things tend to blow up in your face. Hopefully, by reading this book, you will nimbly sidestep that fate.

Let me be clear. I'm not trying to put an engine in the car, I'm trying to fine-tune the engine that we already have. If we can slightly reduce the error rate and the friction, then maybe we can increase economic productivity and efficiency by a smidgen. Every little bit will help, particularly when viewed over the long term. Small percentage differences in annual GDP growth can add up over a twenty- or thirty-year period to a significant difference in our standard of living.

CHAPTER 1
The Business Idea

Any business starts with an idea. *You need a product or service to sell to a target market at a price they are willing to pay.* It is important to consider your purpose in doing so, however. If your purpose is merely to make money, you might not have enough dedication to see things through. If your purpose is to help people, that might inspire you to persevere through the roller-coaster ride of running a business in an ever-changing market. In the broadest sense, the purpose of business is to help people by adding value to their lives, and for some businesspeople it becomes a mission. Given that 50 percent of businesses fail in the first five years, entrepreneurship is not something to be undertaken lightly. Some studies show that the key trait of successful entrepreneurs is perseverance. Calvin Coolidge summed it up well: "Nothing in this world can take the place of persistence. Talent will not; nothing is more common than unsuccessful men with talent. Genius will not; unrewarded genius is almost a proverb. Education will not; the world is full of educated derelicts. Persistence and determination alone are omnipotent."

And I would refine that further. Ancient philosophies like Stoicism, Buddhism, and Hinduism teach "equanimity," which I think is the key trait for anyone running a small business to have. You must be able to remain calm through all the ups and downs. You have to keep the faith. Unflappability, optimism, and a good dose of stubbornness are highly recommended. Many businesspeople start businesses that grow out of their prior careers or side activities (e.g., a hobby). What happens is that they get very good at doing something, and people start asking for their help more and more. For example, I knew a nurse who cared for the elderly who was asked by her clients to do more, and she started an elder care company. However, others do something novel, such as Kevin Plank, the clever and industrious fellow who started Under Armour. Plank had an idea that grew out of his previous experience (football), but he had no experience in executing that type of business (apparel).

Adding value means that one must either find a need and fill it or build a better mousetrap. Often, because some areas of the market are fully developed (insurance is a good example), it is difficult to be a new entrant. Sometimes you can follow the maxim in the movie *Field of Dreams* that "If you build it, they will come." When Steve Jobs and Apple put out the iPhone, that was an example of creating a new market. Before that, people didn't think they would need such a thing because it didn't even exist. But Steve Jobs is the exception. The way markets usually work is this: "If they want it, then you built it." Demand precedes supply. For mature businesses, growth often relies more on entering new markets across the globe than on creating new products or services to sell. A good test is to think forward into the marketing phase. How will you differentiate your offering from that of your competitors? You don't want to confront that question only after you have sunk big money into developing or implementing your business idea.

The tricky part for any business is maintaining its competitive advantage over the long term. If you have a good idea, it usually isn't difficult for someone to copy it and beat you at your own game. At one time, RC, now long gone, was a top cola in the market. Conversely, if you get a chance to visit the Boeing plant near Seattle, it is worth the trip. You will witness the kind of competitive advantage that is not easy to duplicate. If I start up Lloyd's Hawaiian Aircraft Manufacturer, the enterprise will die quickly. The only thing you can be certain of is that the market will change over time. Many ancient philosophies from both the East and West took the transience of earthly existence for granted, and if anything, technology may have accelerated that process.

In formulating your business ideas, don't assume that they have to be big, grandiose ideas. Incremental improvements can also generate cash. Nickel-and-diming is a classic way to make money. Check out the neighborhood convenience store or those inexplicable recurring charges on your phone bill. That stuff can add up over time.

People sometimes worry that others may steal their ideas. Personally, I would rather have my ideas vetted by a few people so that I can get proper feedback. That is one benefit of writing a business plan and asking a bank or venture capitalist for financing instead of just running up a bill on your own credit card. Given the failure rate of new businesses mentioned earlier, it may be advisable to get a second opinion.

I often have ideas for businesses that I can't take advantage of because I am not positioned to do so. What do I do with these ideas? I give them away to businesspeople who are positioned to take advantage of them. Why not? If it makes for a better world, and I live in that world, doesn't this help me?

The key thing to remember is that being in business is not just a matter of having an idea; it is mainly a matter of execution. If I have an idea to start a hamburger restaurant, but I'm a terrible cook and I put too much salt on the beef, then the idea isn't going to work. If I have an idea to start a copy center, but I can't keep the copy machines in good working order, then I'm going to fail. Execution matters. Details matter. Business is not theory, it is practice— implementation, operationalization, craftsmanship. Or as Thomas Edison put it: "Vision without execution is hallucination."

To be blunt, you have to be darn good at something. That goal, however, must be tempered by a sense of reality about your capabilities. As Jim Collins put it: "A Hedgehog Concept is not a goal to be the best, a strategy to be the best, an intention to be the best, a plan to be the best. It is an *understanding* of what you *can* be the best at. This distinction is absolutely crucial" (*Good to Great:*

Why Some Companies Make the Leap … and Others Don't
[Harper Business, 2001], page 98). In other words, hard
work leads to skill, but there may be an outer limit given
one's own innate talent. As noted earlier, if you're not a
computer programmer, perhaps you shouldn't go into a
business that requires IT programming innovation. That
said, because the brain can develop somewhat over time,
you don't really know up front what your skill level will
end up being if you work at it over the long term. It's just
that one has to be realistic about the competition that one
will face.

Of course products need to be vigorously tested, but
remember that even in the design phase a CEO should be
empirical and "kick the tires." You cannot delegate away
completely the task of figuring out whether your product
is attractive and usable by the customer. My secretary
once bought a recording machine that had buttons called
"Talk" and "Listen." Personally, I prefer the standard
labels of "Record" and "Play." But to figure that out, you
have to go look and see for yourself. Don't just sit in the
big corner office staring at the data reports flashing before
your eyes on your computer screen.

Be aware of the question of scalability. Some businesses
are brick-and-mortar and tied to specific pieces of real
estate. Others can easily scale up to a very large size,
even to a global operation. The fact that a business is
not scalable doesn't mean that you shouldn't do it; it just
means that you want to go in with your eyes open about
how big the potential is down the road. Some businesses

do well over a lifetime just by staying small. Getting big can be good, but it also has a downside.

It pays to look below the surface when analyzing an existing business. At first blush, McDonald's appears to be a restaurant business, but because they buy land underneath the restaurant and lease it back to franchisees, they are also a real estate business and a financing business. Similarly, while higher education appears to be about training young minds for the workforce, it is also about research and development for potential business uses. In a larger sense, it is an economic development business. Another example is Fox News/Fox Business, which looks like a news organization but is also partly in the entertainment business.

Observe the difference between upside risk and downside risk. It can sometimes be tempting to go after a big possible upside, but if doing so involves a big possible downside, you should sleep on it. If you can find something with a big possible upside and a relatively limited downside, that might be more attractive. All business involves a roll of the dice, but there is a difference between taking a calculated risk and gambling like a drunken fool.

Finally, let me tell you what I consider a good compliment. It's nice when someone says: "Hey, Lloyd, that's a good idea"; but it's far better if they say: "Hey, Lloyd, that's a good tool." See the difference? Going one step beyond the idea into implementation. Not just thinking, but doing. Or at least starting to.

CHAPTER **2**

Relationships

Someone once told me that "business is about relationships." That is often true. You have to have friends. I don't mean "friends" in the sense of someone you would go camping with or go to the movies with on Saturday night. I mean an acquaintance with whom you are basically on good terms and can have an affable conversation. It is not just a matter of having good relations with your customers or your employees or your bankers; it is a question of knowing and exchanging information with people all over your community so that you know what is going on around you. None of us can be expert in everything, so if you have a wide range of friends with different expertise, you can use them as a resource at the same time that you can be a resource for them.

In our modern world of handheld computer devices and electronic communications, I fear that we might be losing the art of the business lunch. I like business lunches because they build relationships and are a great way of exchanging information on an informal basis for which there is no written record. When things go into the written record, people are less likely to be candid. That said, no conversation is private because what you say can be repeated. But when you deal with sophisticated people, they usually know better than to do that to you. If you don't want reciprocal disclosure, then you must provide reciprocal confidentiality.

The bottom line is that in an information-based society where most of what we sell are services, you must understand the value of human intelligence. And by that I don't mean smarts, I mean "intelligence" in the way that a spy thinks of it—information known only to a few. Another important aspect of business relationships is that when I am looking for a new vendor, I usually ask my business acquaintances for a referral. If you know a lot of people and you have a good reputation, it is easier to find quality vendors.

In addition, talking to people is part of the standard reality testing that we all do to correct our own thinking. A person who spends too much time alone can end up in a private world of discourse, playing with a glass menagerie, if you will. A key element of any relationship is reciprocity. If someone does something nice for you, you should remember it and try to return the favor one day. If you don't, and you develop a reputation for being ungrateful, then people will not have much of an incentive to help you. We all need help from time to time. In other words, being altruistic can be a good evolutionary trait, and is not just a matter of being religious or being a dupe like some people think. Anyway, even if I am nice most of the time, that doesn't mean that I am not capable of being a jerk when I choose to be. Most of the better businesspeople I know go out of their way to be polite.

I talked about reciprocity. If we go back to the Bible, the entire value system is based on the idea of a covenant. Not "You scratch my back; I scratch yours," which sounds like corruption. A covenant is an agreement for mutually beneficial behavior by both parties that is based mostly on trust and must not be breached. That idea is the foundation for any society. For those who think this kind of thinking is too legalistic, perhaps it is better just to say that empathy can help in business if it enables you to see things as others do. Have you ever helped someone who turned right around and stabbed you in the back, and then the very next day they acted like they were your best buddy? We all have, and they make for cruddy businesspeople—at least in the long run.

CHAPTER 3

Client Management and Customer Service

To define my terms, although these are essentially the same thing, I think of a *client* as pertaining more to a licensed professional or a consultant, as distinct from a *customer*, which could be any buyer in an ordinary retail service setting. One can go on forever with anecdotes and axioms about customer service, but the big picture question is how to get a customer to be willing to promote your firm to one of his or her friends or business acquaintances. Or for a lesser standard, how do you get a customer to refrain from bad-mouthing your firm all over the place? Because you don't want to get into a downward death spiral. Hopefully, if you take care of your customers, they'll take care of you.

Part A: Client Management

A service vendor has a special relationship problem: the management of client expectations. Honesty and disclosure up front are helpful; this approach is sometimes called transparency. As my college friend put it, there are six basic guidelines to follow: (a) listen to what your client has to say; (b) tell the client specifically and clearly what you are going to do and not going to do; (c) explain the downsides, the risks, and the uncertainties to your approach; (d) do what you say you are going to do; (e) know which decisions belong to the client and don't try to decide for them, and (f) tell the client what you did and did not do. Most importantly, you have to *listen* to your clients in order to get an understanding of their needs and the possibilities that exist for making them more successful at their own businesses.

Most vendors have many clients and a lot of work to do, so no client intelligently expects the vendor to remember up-to-the-minute details of their situation. Some people have a good memory, and some don't. But if there is an e-mail or correspondence history, particularly if you don't have a good memory or you are busy on many other things, it is highly advisable to go back and look at some of the recent e-mail history with a client *before* you speak to that client again. For example, you don't want to keep asking the client the same question over and over when it has been asked and answered. In addition, clients normally are going through time lines and procedures that may be largely outside your knowledge, so to avoid getting in the client's way, you may want to check some of the recent e-mail history before you take action with respect to that client. It takes you an extra minute, but if it helps you avoid wasting your client's time, then isn't that time well spent?

The old saying was that the customer was always right. Is that true? Not necessarily, but of course if you try to save customers from themselves, it must be done with great sensitivity and awareness of the risks. A lot of times as a client I will say, "I have been so advised," just to let the vendor off the hook. What's the problem with just doing wrong things at the client's request? Later on, the client might conveniently forget that you had advised them properly and blame you anyway. Conversely, if you saved a client from a problem who realizes it down the road, that client will speak very well of you. Many vendors have a bit of a financial conflict of interest with their clients, but if you consider the importance of your long-term reputation and don't put making a fast buck about the best interests of your client, that might be the best course of action. Building trust in the community often involves developing a reputation for ethics, character, good faith, and fair dealing.

One of the hardest things to do is to follow up on loose ends with your client. Sometimes a good deal of time may elapse between contacts. Perhaps one day, all computers will have an automatic system for vendors that immediately locates the last communication with a given client and creates ticklers to flag the need to follow up. As I said earlier, no one can remember every little thing, but it is easy for a faulty memory to be taken as incompetence or stupidity when it is not. So it is up to you what kind of impression you want to create.

That said, my pet peeve in client relations is the impatient vendor who can't wait for the client to respond in a reasonable time frame. Eager beavers who are "just following up" are *pests*. Let me suggest that a good businessperson may not want to be seen as a pest. You don't "follow up" unless the time that has elapsed suggests that your client may have forgotten. If you are contacting the client before the decision has been made, then you are being pushy. It's not rocket science. The words *follow up* imply "after." Dazzle your clients by understanding the meaning of simple words. In fact, this paragraph is derived from a real-life example, and do you know that this so-called "business development" officer keep leaving messages on my phone after I had issued him an e-mail saying that we weren't going to use his firm? Gee, can we all ponder for a moment whether a sociopath is really the best kind of person to do sales? Are you a salesperson or a stalker?

I discuss the importance of not accusing clients of owing you money unless they actually do in a later chapter. That is to say, do you know on any given day what your client has paid you and the outstanding balance due? I mean, without asking your client?

Now let me clue you in to a little trick to giving advice. The wrong way is to spew personal opinions all over the place. The right way is to provide objective facts. People have the right to make their own decisions about their destiny, but often they have incomplete information, and this is the source of error. Just give people the right few relevant facts, and watch them go! To put it another way, in law there is a big difference between merely stating what a statute says and offering a legal opinion about how and whether the law applies to a given fact pattern. As you move from the first to the second, you more toward the giving of actual advice, and that is where liability can arise. In addition, note that sometimes argumentation can be done in a diplomatic way by asking questions instead of making assertions. Getting people to think for themselves is often more helpful and respectful than spoon-feeding them like children.

It's a good idea to have some empathy for your client (i.e., thoughtfulness). You don't want to do something that creates unnecessary issues, and in particular you don't want to embarrass your client. Here's an example. A law firm drafted a document for a meeting that I was chairing. Because of my computer security protocols, I asked my sister to print out the document. She did, and I picked it up from her office and copied it for the meeting. At the meeting I found out that it wasn't the right version, which caused a process problem and damaged my leadership credibility just a tiny bit. Why did this happen? Because the lawyer who drafted the document didn't put a draft date on it—you know, like: "draft no. 2, dated February 17, 2017." For a lawyer to make this kind of error is not the optimal professional standard for which we strive. It is these kinds of small errors in the inception that can snowball and create larger problems downstream.

Now, everyone is busy, and sometimes things take longer to do than one predicts, and sometimes things go wrong unexpectedly. Some vendors want to hide such problems from their clients, but the danger is that when the problem blows up in your client's face, you don't want it to be a surprise. Sometimes if you are having a problem and you disclose it to your client, they can help work out a solution before the explosion happens. But these kinds of workarounds, which are common, require lead time to implement. As I said earlier, many vendors do not have a complete understanding of their client's time line and objectives or of the consequences of a failure to meet the time line. So think in terms of open communication. Even if you don't care about your client, try to make it look like you do.

Part B: Customer Service

Now on to ordinary retail "customers." There is a twenty-four-hour diner that I go to at least three times a week, usually around 1 or 2 a.m., and I am a heavy tipper. So I go there one night, and the place is only about one-third full, and the waiter tries to seat me at the counter. Normally, the waitresses offer me whatever seat I want. So here's the question: Do you want to recognize a regular customer or treat a regular the same way as tourist trade that you'll probably never see again? Hmmmm, let's puzzle that one out, shall we?

Then I go there two nights later, again at 1 a.m., and the guy does the same thing to me, only this time the restaurant is less than 10 percent full. So this time I complain to the other waitresses about what a horse's arse this guy is. I'm not trying to get him fired—I get that I am privileged in a way that he is not. I'm trying to help the business do better and thereby help the people that work there (caveat: that only works when you're right—I have occasionally been wrong in my criticisms, and boy is that embarrassing, although it not a bad way to learn). By the way, do you know how those errors in criticism I personally make usually start? They start out, "I'm a lawyer, so I know …." Pride goeth before a fall. To put it another way, instead of going at a vendor and saying, "You messed me up," try starting with a question like "Why is it this way?" Less confrontational.

Here's another one in the same vein. I go to a grocery store that is part of a national chain, and I offer the checkout clerk my smartcard which they use to track my purchases. She says, "I'll take it over here." So instead of my standing on the left side of the bar-code scanner, I have to move to the right side. This is a walk of maybe seven inches. Now, if I were her boss, I would fire her on the spot because she is on a power trip about how she wants things her way. What the heck is the difference whether you take the card from one side of the keyboard or the other? Every other checkout clerk there takes my card the other way. Am I not the customer, and don't I have a basic human right to not get bossed around by a petty tyrant dressed as a checkout clerk who is making up arbitrary rules?

Also, remember that to give customers a break requires some latitude. If workers don't have a little discretion, they can sometimes be too rigid when dealing with customers. In other words, if you create a work environment where workers can get in trouble for being nice, that can create a problem. That doesn't mean that you give away the store or don't have rules; it just means that sometimes situations arise that require judgment, and if a manager isn't there to resolve it, then the worker must. It is similar to the relationship between our courts and our cops. The cops are the front line, and they have to make legal judgments all the time right there on the street to resolve matters long before they even get to a court.

When hiring people who will face the public, make sure they are good listeners and can learn as they go. Customers are not always right, but they ought to be listened to, and their side of the story needs to be researched and considered. Customer service requires training because such workers are half teacher and half social worker. When I was in the government, I answered the information inquiries despite being the administrator because I saw it as our opportunity to have a positive impact on our public image by looking knowledgeable. I didn't see it as a low level task for a drone.

One thing a customer service representative must do is grasp quickly what the customer is asking. I have been on a call where it took me over five minutes to get the customer service representative to admit that they couldn't do what I needed done. That's irritating, and it makes the company look stupid. On another call, I had a customer service person for an online retailer refuse to help me because in taking my address for security purposes, she wanted the extra four numbers that come after the normal five of the zip code, even though virtually nobody carries that information in their heads. I told her: "Do you know that I have spent many thousands of dollars on this site in the past year?" What a great way to lose an outstanding customer.

Another time I went into a bank to open an account for a trust and before I could finish explaining my situation, the banker was talking over me and telling me things. I said: "don't you want to find out what I'm trying to tell you, before you start making decisions?" This is an example of a younger fellow who probably spends most of his time writing into a handheld device. Human interaction means listening. And maybe he should have checked first to see if I was already a customer at that bank? Here's a pet peeve—waiters/waitresses or cashiers at food service establishments who try to guess your order before you say it because they have seen you there before. Don't get ahead of yourself. Just listen. No one is asking you to be a mind reader. It doesn't prove your brilliance to pretend to read minds, you know?

When using a largely automated canned computer response to customer service issues, beware the danger of the bad fit. You don't want a canned computer message to keep telling your customers that they are wrong and stupid in the way they are doing things unless they actually are. The computer canned response needs to be recognized as the blunt instrument it is. Whatever you do, don't keep blaming your customers for not understanding how to use your computer system unless you are very sure that this allegation is correct and that there is nothing wrong on your end.

Many computer systems do have bugs in them. Here's a good story about an IT firm. Decades ago I had a minor software issue, and I got a personal phone call from the CEO and inventor of the software. Boy, that was fun, and I will always remember it. He understood the importance of making his customers feel important and of customizing his customer service response. Sure, he was an expert computer programmer and probably super rich, but he didn't let that get in the way of having the human touch.

Conceptually, ask yourself why we put effort into customer service. Is it just to get whiny customers to shut up? Or is it to help our business improve so that we can make more money? It is human nature for customer service people to get defensive when criticized, but some of us who put extra effort into giving businesses feedback are doing so because we are trying to help Team USA.

Now, all that said, at some point if a client becomes enough of a problem, and you are not at fault, you don't have to take garbage from spoiled consumers forever. Americans are used to brilliant levels of quality service that people in some other countries would regard as magical. I do believe that I have a general duty as a customer to be nice and patient. However, I also believe that I have a duty to society at large to at least feign anger when someone does something so far below any professional standard that calling it "stupid" would be a compliment. I am forgiving of people because I know how hard business can be, but we all should make a continual effort to rise above mediocrity, don't you agree? The key is knowing the difference between a customer who is trying to give you constructive feedback and a customer who is a troublemaker.

CHAPTER 4

Reading—Someone's Got to Do It

A favorite joke that floats around the Hawaii State Legislature is "In the land of the blind, the one eyed man is king." People often don't like to read, partly because they're often slow at it and partly because they're too busy or too lazy. Alan Kay pointed out that human beings are not naturally inclined by evolutionary processes to read. Who is Alan Kay? He, along with Doug Englebart, invented the graphical user interface around 1968. Do you know how I know that? I read a book on the history of inventions. Almost everyone thinks that Steve Jobs created the graphical interface. If you don't read, then there won't be correct facts in your head for your brain to operate on, and no matter how smart you are, it is going to be tough to get things right.

Reading broadly in various subject areas is also important because reconciling conflicting information is how we develop our critical thinking. As Fran Lebowitz put it: "Think before you speak. Read before you think." Let me give a simple example. For over a decade I watched people on television talking about discrimination against Islam. So here's my question: how many of these people have read the Koran and at least two histories of the Middle East? I did that because I considered it the bare minimum diligence on the topic. I even read *The Koran for Dummies* to double-check my own reading. And by the way, when I say "history," I mean "written by a historian with a PhD in history who works or has worked in the history or religion department of an accredited university," not Glenn Beck or someone else without an adequate foundation. Consider the question of whether the words "Christianity," "Judaism," "Islam" and "Hinduism," are equivalent "religions." How can a person know if they don't know the doctrine underneath each of those labels? I'm not trying to be political, I'm trying to encourage people not to judge a book by its cover.

I have read many books, but I also read magazines, including *The Economist, Bloomberg Businessweek, Fortune, Scientific American,* the *MIT Technology Review,* and *Foreign Affairs.* In addition, I skim the daily newspaper and flip back and forth across various cable news channels (but particularly Fox Business and Bloomberg's). These sources help me feel comfortable that I have a rough sense of current events so that I don't make too many mistakes when I speak or write.

When I was younger, I was accused of having my head in the clouds and not paying attention to what was going on around me. Someone said: "A businessman has to know what is going on around him." That is a fair point. We all have to stay current. Books can save us time. For example, I once wanted to create a list of good music quotes. I skimmed a book by one of my former professors, who was a pianist and musicologist. It took me only an hour to pull about a dozen really nice quotes from the book, but it probably took him many years to survey the entire scope of Western literature in order to create that book. I'll say it again: books can create efficiency, if they are good books. Now, of course, there are many bad books, and even good books may contain a lot of bad information. One has to be able to sift the wheat from the chaff. Books are not the be-all and end-all. But they are an important tool and, if used right, can create efficiency.

Here's a hot tip: some things can be browsed or speed-read, at least for a first pass (there is no law against rereading as many times as needed). But to do that you have to have read with a purpose. That is to say, you must be looking for something. Note that not everything can be browsed. With fiction or history, for example, you may have to read every single word. Now, speed-reading doesn't happen on day one, but the more reading you do and the more information you already know, the easier it will be to speed-read.

Now some executives like to hear it from others, either verbally or by way of a concise summary. That may be necessary, but one must always be aware that not reading the original text necessarily means that you aren't getting the whole story and that you may be subject to the error or subterfuge of the person you are relying upon. Things tend to get lost in translation.

CHAPTER 5

Cost Control Is a Two-Edged Sword

We all know that to make a profit, revenues must exceed expenses. Because expanding revenues can be a real uphill battle, there is often an incentive to reduce costs. This is okay, but only up to a point. If you reduce costs so much that the quality of your product or service is adversely affected, then you can hurt yourself. That is why a good business professor doesn't tell you that your only objective is profits. He or she tells you that your primary objective is to "maximize revenue." Take a look at Amazon. They went for a long time without profits. Their focus was growing their market share and reinvesting in the business.

You need to know the difference between general inflation and price increases within a given industry or with a given product. Inflation is a monetary phenomenon that is a function of currency and the overall quantity of goods and services produced in a country. Price increases in a given industry or with a given product or service are usually mostly a function of supply and demand. Now, not to insult anyone's intelligence, but prices are what a seller charges the buyer, and while those prices are costs to the buyer, the costs to a seller are typically less than the prices that seller charges. In other words, many sellers use cost-plus pricing so they can make sure they earn a profit. That may seem obvious, and I wish it were, but I have seen supposedly top-level people on television conflate prices with costs.

Fixed costs are those you have regardless of the number of units that you sell. *Variable costs* are those that increase or decrease as the number of units you sell increases or decreases.

A *sunk cost* is a concept from economics. The idea is that once a cost is in the past—once the money is spent and gone—you shouldn't allow that to affect your decisions about what to do next. As an example, at some point you may realize that something you're working on isn't going to bear fruit. At that point you should cut your losses and stop doing it. As the old saying goes: "Don't throw good money after bad." The hard part is that once your ego is invested in a course of action, it can be hard to admit that you screwed up and lit a pile of money on fire. Regrettably, that happens more than it should. I have seen foolish leaders double and triple down on their bad decisions with even worse decisions in order to make it look as if the original bad decision was right when it was actually demonstrably not so. To be blunt, that doesn't make things better. Everyone makes mistakes, so who cares if you do now and then? Admit it, fold your tent, and move on. They say a winner never quits? Tell that to the Board of Directors of Yahoo. I'll bet the wished they had sold the business two years earlier because it would have been worth far more.

Also note that politicians often assume incorrectly that a business can pass all of its costs on to the consumers. Sometimes there is a limit to how much you can raise your price and still sell enough to cover your costs. In addition, observe that the price of your product or service is in a wholly different market from the costs of running your business. For example, if you sell chocolate chip cookies, there may be competition that drives down the prices of those cookies, but that doesn't mean that your electric bill is going to go down. If a business cannot pass costs along, then it can affect things like the wages paid to the employees who work in the business, which has downstream effects on the economy.

When putting someone in charge of spending decisions, including yourself, you might want to create a process with some checks and balances. The reason is that every person has a slightly different relationship to money. Some people are spendthrifts; they get a thrill out of spending money. Other people are misers; they get a thrill out of hoarding money. Some people are gamblers; others take calculated risks; while still others are completely risk averse. Going to extremes in either direction can be bad for business, although it depends on the case at hand. The psychological aspect of money is just something you need to bear in mind. I will say more on this in a future chapter.

If one is starting a business for the first time, doing a realistic budget projection is crucial. It is easy to miss certain costs of doing business, such as payroll taxes, insurance costs, and IT service expenses. In addition, learning about the details of payroll is important, which is why some businesses use the services of specialized vendors to help them with this and other aspects related to having employees. In addition, most businesses will buy insurance in the form of a standard business owner's policy (BOP) which has a variety of coverages, but at a minimum you need liability insurance. Why? As an example, our family business got sued by a woman who claimed that she hurt her hand getting a soda out of the soda machine. Lawyers sue because their clients want them to, and they only need to have a good faith argument under the law or, in federal court, meet the standard of plausibility. Lawyers do not have to believe that they are actually going to win, and most cases settle before trial anyway.

Finally, watch out for the "cost-control sprite." What is that? It is the spirit or force or karmic finger that touches you when you act like too much of a skinflint or cheapskate. Here's an example. The ceremony for the award of the CPCU was held at a very nice hotel which I had not been to before. My mother suggested that I use the valet parking. I got there and saw that the valet was over five dollars, so I decided to park in the hotel parking lot. We had a nice ceremony, and I got my little piece of paper. But I had parked next to a wall, a bit too close, and when I was pulling out of the parking space, I turned too soon and the wall "interacted" with my the doors on the left side of my car. In the end, I spent over a thousand dollars to replace the two doors. Talk about being penny-wise and pound-foolish! Sound superstitious? Yep, and I avoid walking under ladders too. Our economy runs mostly on spending; it runs on savings only to a lesser extent. When you are in business, you should accept with a light heart that there is always a cost of doing business. Pay it forward.

CHAPTER 6

Long-Term versus Short-Term Thinking

John Maynard Keynes once famously said, "In the long run, we are all dead." So what's his point? That nothing matters? Just stop doing anything? Just do whatever? I'm not sure that this was a very meaningful statement.

We all have to get through the short term in order to reach the long term. Everyone knows that. But if you engage in bad behavior toward your customers in the short term, there may not be a long term. I have seen people do this because they think of their business as a series of one-shot deals, sort of like a series of one night stands, "wham, bam, thank you, ma'am." Personally, I think this approach is foolish because it assumes that people don't talk. Sure, it can be hard for information to flow quickly or evenly to everyone in a given market. But I don't think it is wise to assume permanent secrecy in a world of electronic communications, social media, and cell phones with video cameras.

My experience is that when someone acts badly, people talk and talk. I like to play the long game and think of all people as potentially coming back at me later in life.

Because they do sometimes. Some call it karma; others call it the Holy Spirit at work the world. Whatever you call it, it is bad business to disappoint people. As the old saying goes: It takes a lifetime to build a reputation, but only five minutes to lose it. A quick example will suffice. A vendor did some work for me and, after I paid, sent me a big refund due to an overpayment which I was not aware of. Now, if anyone asks me about them, I will say, "They did a nice job, and they're honest people." That's how goodwill gets built, and it has value.

Someone once told me about the *New York Times* rule, which is simply that if you wouldn't want your behavior or words printed on the front page of the newspaper, then don't do it (or say it). Putting it plainly, don't assume that the things you do will remain hidden. You're not invisible. The walls have ears. The fact is that when you do something indefensible, you will tend to lie about it, and quite often that's where the real damage to your credibility is done. The underlying infraction may be relatively forgettable, but lying to the public is often not forgettable because people aren't generally stupid enough to believe those lies in the first place. There is an insult-to-intelligence element that is inherently bad public relations.

Another aspect of short-term versus long-term thinking is what might be called either the snowballing effect, the cascade effect, or the domino effect of a bad decision. One bad decision tends to cause a chain of bad effects that spirals out of control. So one must look ahead to the long-term effects and not merely the "crisis du jour."

CHAPTER 7

SWOT Analysis and Strategic Planning

A simple tool for strategic planning is the SWOT analysis, or the analysis of Strengths, Weaknesses, Opportunities, and Threats. The first two are a look inside your organization (or self). The second two are a look outside. Internal view; external view. Basically, you make a list or, if you want, a four-box grid with lists inside of them. The benefit of periodically doing a SWOT analysis is that we as humans all have difficulty seeing ourselves objectively, and this method can help us get outside ourselves.

A SWOT is part of strategic planning. Strategic planning is the process of taking stock of where you are, setting your goals and targets, and then figuring out how to make them happen. Planning always involves conjecture, and that uncertainty argues against dotting every *i* and crossing every *t* in your strategic plan. As the poet put it, the best-laid plans of mice and men often go awry.

A good businessperson is constantly thinking about the future anyway, so there is an artificial aspect to this kind of "consultant flow chart" exercise. For example, even though a formal SWOT analysis might be done only periodically, I for one am poring over media every day to see what is happening. I do SWOT analysis almost every day unconsciously, and I'm sure that most businesspeople do, regardless of whether they went to business school or not.

Do you know what a "gap analysis" is? It is an assessment of the "gap" between where you are today and where you want to be. That alone doesn't answer the question of how you get from one to the other, but it is one important step in the preliminary stages of a change initiative.

People in an organization know a lot about what they do, but they often have a blind spot. People outside the organization don't know much, but some might have perspective because of distance. So a smart leader will be willing to hear input from inside and outside, to the extent possible. Of course, listening doesn't mean that you take all the advice that you get; sifting the good from the bad requires judgment. But remember: "out of the mouths of babes" and "kids say the darnedest things." That is to say, don't judge the quality of advice by the speaker's suit because, frankly, there are a lot of empty suits out there running around.

Compensation policy is part of business strategy. Obviously if you pay more, you may be able to attract better talent, although money is not the only thing people respond to. Incentive pay, otherwise known as pay for performance, works, but you need an objective way of measuring performance that can't be gamed by either the worker or a manager. I happen to like a flat salary because I am fast, and I like getting done with my work fast so that I can have some downtime. Billable hours tend to favor people who work slowly. I always meet people who claim to be very busy, but sometimes it is more that they are slow.

By the way, not all downtime is bad. Downtime provides an opportunity for reflection and creativity. People who always have their noses to the grindstone sometimes lose perspective. Also, and I will discuss this more in depth later, remember that having an incentive pay scheme in place does not relieve you of the day-to-day duties of a manager.

Strategic planning is not just about the "value-proposition" underlying your business; it is also about values, as in ethical or social values. The two ideas are sometimes related.

Although implementation and execution may not technically be part of strategic planning, time lines are. You must always give yourself enough time to do something, at least to the extent possible. Tasks and processes tend to take longer than expected, and the longer time line you have to work within, the easier it is to figure out what needs to be done and to deal with problems as they arise. If you put yourself into a fire drill, not only will the error rate go up, but so will the stress level for you and everyone else working on the project.

Part of establishing the right time line is the idea of the "critical path." The point is that the old adage "First things first" isn't always correct. What happens in real life is that sometimes you can't do something (X) until something else is completed first (Y). If that is the case, then even if it seems like X goes before Y, you may have to start working on Y simultaneously so that you don't create a delay down the road. In other words, if possible, your time line shouldn't create a situation where people are just sitting around waiting for something to happen.

Murphy's Law holds that if anything can go wrong, it will and (Finnegan's Corollary) at the worst possible time. So how do you mitigate this problem? By giving yourself a longer time line. In addition, spending the first part of that time line thinking about the right approach to the project is likely to be time well spent.

If your business is brick and mortar, think not just about location but about ample parking. Also, be aware that the size, layout, and setup of your brick-and-mortar space will have an effect on your customers and your workers. There is a FedEx-Kinko's center not far from my residence, and the interior is so great that I just like being inside the store. I'm there maybe twice a week.

Although standard business decisions are not strategic planning, you need strategic planning to figure out how to approach the standard decision making process. No one ever has complete information when making a decision. There is always uncertainty as to the future. But one has to judge in each situation what quantum of information should be looked at before making the decision and what procedure should be used. With some kinds of decisions, if you follow an order of operations or sequence, you will have a better chance to detect errors. Checks and balances are sometimes a good idea. During the Cuban missile crisis, President Kennedy picked someone to act as a "devil's advocate" in the meetings. I think that was smart.

Some people make a hard distinction between big-picture thinking and detail work. Actually, the two are intimately related. If you try to make big-picture strategic decisions without grasping certain key details, the entire decision may go wrong. In my view, while it is true that some detail-oriented people can't see the big picture, many can, and of the two, detail work is often the more arduous task.

Some people focus on the goal of maximizing shareholder value, but that is too narrow. A business owner or manager has many stakeholders. In addition to shareholders, there are customers, employees, lenders, vendors, politicians and government regulators, and the community at large. In the old days it was traditional for business leaders to do philanthropy. It is not just a matter of not looking like a selfish, money-grubbing user. Many of the problems we face as a society are interconnected, and it is likely that some of the challenges faced by your business are related to other challenges in society. By doing things that show that you understand that, you might help yourself by setting a good example for others and thereby acting as a force multiplier.

A key strategic question is whether you have to become more like your competitors in order to compete with them or whether you want to strongly differentiate yourself. There isn't a perfect decision rule about this—it may end up being some of both—but usually you have to retain some kind of differentiation to compete in the market.

Another key question is whether you want to stay small or get bigger, which is related to the question of whether you want to focus on a narrow scope of products or services like Coca-Cola or you want to cover the waterfront with a diversified portfolio of products like Proctor & Gamble. There is not necessarily a right answer. It depends on your situation. Remember that while adaptation and opportunism can be good, there is some risk in getting too far away from your core competency and main source of competitive advantage. In addition, don't be fooled by size. Big doesn't necessarily mean profitable or solvent. Big debt can turn a big business into a big problem. In law, some of the smartest lawyers are sole practitioners because, being smart and dominant, they find it difficult to partner with other lawyers.

Finally, a word on the strategic importance of certain "separations." Life is full of conflicts of interest, and to combat the corruption that can result from them, we establish certain lines, called "firewalls" or "Chinese walls." We like to separate the function of signing checks from the filling out of the blanks on the checks and the accounting for the expenditures. We like to separate the marketing people from the risk management people. We like to separate the government from the establishment of religion. We like to separate civilian control of the government from the military. We like to separate the political layer of government at the top which is subject to elections from the professional class below. We separate the legislative, judicial, and executive branches from each other. We separate the investigation of wrongdoing from the decision to undertake a prosecution.

These separations are critical to avoiding corruption and bad decision-making. It is not understatement to say that they are the foundation for the success of our system. So watch out for people who are trying to consolidate personal power and blur these kinds of lines, because they are idiots who are plainly incapable of strategic thinking. Don't be one of them. Now as to the separation between the federal and state governments and the separation between government and business, the jury is still out on how far the lines can be blurred. I don't like any blur, but that's me. I don't assume that most people can be selfless, and it is wiser not to put them in a situation where they will be overly tempted.

Meetings

Meetings are often a huge waste of people's time. Remember that if seven people are in attendance, a one-hour meeting is not just one lost hour. You just lost seven hours of productivity. See, e.g., Jason Fried and David Heinemeier Hansson, *Rework* (Crown Business, 2010), page 109.

Therefore, if you are going to have a meeting, the leader of that meeting needs to put enough time and effort into preparation so that the meeting can be as short as possible. Getting your thoughts into an efficient format takes more effort than most people realize. It not only requires creating an agenda. Ideally you should write out what you are going to say so that you don't meander all over the place. That doesn't mean that you sit there in the meeting and read what you have written word for word. It means that your "extemporaneous" speech will tend to be better if the thoughts have been rehearsed. If you think about it, people that hold meetings without preparation are arrogant because they think they have a right to waste people's time. Such people usually like to hear themselves talk, even when they are droning on about nothing and making themselves look foolish.

One should also realize the basic fact that if you are in a meeting discussing things, you can't at the same time be doing research on legal or financial or factual questions. That's why you often want to figure out the issues before the meeting and do a little research so that there can be actual progress at the meeting. Of course not all issues can be anticipated, but it can be helpful to show forward momentum as you progress from meeting to meeting; going around and around endlessly raising issues can really slow you down. Also, when working with a board, you don't want to hand out documents at the meeting. The board members will want to read the packet before they get there so they can think about it in advance. If you blindside a board in a meeting with new information, they will likely blindside you with questions.

The other thing about meetings is that they are often subject to groupthink and undue influence by one person or another, such as a boss. For that reason, if I want to hear opinions, I sometimes just ask people to respond individually to an e-mail or a survey and avoid a meeting altogether.

That said, sometimes there is no substitute for a face-to-face meeting because of the creative way that human interaction can build upon itself. Sometimes the speed of face-to-face back-and-forth communications is needed. But generally meetings should be used sparingly.

CHAPTER 9

Reporting and Data

As to workers reporting to management and middle management reporting to top management, some of that is necessary, but it should be kept to the minimum necessary because time spent reporting is time spent not doing something else. One day, our IT systems will provide operational feedback on a weekly or monthly basis to each employee so they can be self-aware. That will be a good thing, but we are not there quite yet from a technological standpoint. Legacy systems and the costs of their replacement often get in the way.

With the computer age has come a near obsession with data collection and data mining. All well and good, except for the associated time and expense. Don't collect information that you're not going to use. What does that mean? First, as President Obama said about education testing: "Weighing a pig doesn't make it any fatter." In other words, collecting data doesn't mean that it is going to produce a solution. And data without proper interpretation is noise. Second, sometimes we know what to do without much data, even though there is uncertainty. Almost any innovation process involves trial and error. Third, if you haven't properly defined the problem, you might be collecting the wrong data.

Data without a date is meaningless (or misleading). It is rare to find data that isn't at least a bit stale. We call that the "data lag." The point is to be aware that using data, while obviously very important, inherently means that you are looking in the rearview mirror. Also, bear in mind that the period under consideration can affect the kind of trends that a data set reveals. That means that the duration of period under consideration matters, but also note that the past does not always predict the future if the world is changing significantly. Note: the other reason for dating documents containing data or references to data is that it makes the documents easier to authenticate in court (i.e., prove that these documents are the real McCoy).

A word about studies. Business professors often have difficulty doing solid research because they don't have access to internal business data, and the studies end up being more like general social science research, which is better at ferreting out correlation than causation. But you also have to be wary of the fact that when researchers know they have a data problem, they may adjust the research questions so as to sidestep that problem. This in turn may render the study unable to determine the full complexity of the many causes that may be involved in the subject matter of the study. For example, when dealing with human behavior, it is sometimes key to look into intentions, but that isn't always possible because the available data relates to observable behavior more than what is inside someone's head. The larger point is that when reading any study, one must take things with a grain of salt.

One of my favorite moments in film is from *Total Recall.* The villain, the administrator on Mars, played by Ronny Cox, is yelling at his henchman, played by Michael Ironside. Cox says: "Think? I don't give you enough information to think. You just do what you're told. That's what you do."

I don't think this is good management, but too many bosses act this way. They control information because knowledge is power. They believe that to retain control, they must not share information. What's the problem with that? Employees need information, particularly as to the context of the orders they have been given, in order to operate intelligently. A manager who doesn't share information increases his or her own power but usually at the expense of creating dysfunction and mistrust within the organization. The result is often a rising error rate. Now, I realize that nobody has time to tell everybody everything. I realize that division of labor is a big part of why our economies work properly. But I submit that the sharing of relevant information is needed to produce quality results.

As a manager I have fun trying to figure out what someone knows and doesn't know and then giving them a key piece of information and watching them act on it. I don't feel as if I am manipulating them. I like to think that I am helping them achieve their goal, which is to succeed, despite having been compared to both Rasputin and Svengali for doing this sort of thing. To me, people will only act in their perceived self-interest anyway, so I just want them to consider the relevant facts before they run off and do something foolish. Managers that won't share information are usually insecure and trying to erect protectionist barriers around themselves, regardless of the adverse impact to the organization. They don't see that if their approach increases the error rate, their protectionism could have the opposite effect from what they intend.

To avoid sounding overly abstract, let me provide examples of the kinds of holes that can exist in people's knowledge. Do financial advisers know much about the corporate governance of small corporations? Not necessarily, because they usually focus on publicly traded companies. Does an insurance claim adjuster know much about how the insurer's actuary determined the premium rating structure? Not necessarily, because these are two completely separated parts of the insurance company. Does a musician know everything about music history? Not necessarily, because music history is mostly the province of the musicologist. Does a doctor know a lot about the healthcare financing system? Not necessarily, because doctors are taught medicine, not finance. Does an experienced corporate executive know how to handle the media? Not necessarily, because most corporate jobs are hidden behind the façade of the corporation. And so on, and so forth—you see what I mean.

What's the smartest play? Don't wait for others to hand you information on a silver platter; always be on the lookout for new information. If you don't stay current, you can easily become a danger to yourself and others. And if you teach others to do the same, then maybe they will need less spoon-feeding. I'm always amazed by people who say, "I don't need to know that." How can you know whether the information is impactful if you don't know it? Why build barriers around yourself like that? Why make your world smaller?

CHAPTER 11

Misattribution of Causation

I was giving a speech on one of my books, and someone in the audience asked, "If you were to do one thing about education, what would it be?" I replied that I would require every high school to teach the difference between correlation and causation. What is that difference? Nutshell example: When I walk outside, it rains, but that doesn't mean the one caused the other.

We live in a very complex world, what a statistician might call a *multivariate* world (meaning a given outcome is usually the result of many factors). Because of that, it can be difficult to determine the precise cause of our problems. Quite often there is what I like to call "misattribution of causation," which means that people are confusing various happenings with each other. For example, one might observe the relative decline in US power on the world stage and also observe that this coincides with (is correlated with) the rising percentage of nonwhite people in the American citizenry. And one might say: "If we just got rid of those brown and yellow people, everything would be okay again."

Another example of misattribution of causation is when people in the Middle East blame the United States, their "great Satan," for all of their problems, instead of looking inward at the impact that some of their own beliefs are having on their own societies. Another example is when a father in a rural African village thinks his daughter's AIDS is caused by the evil spirits hanging around her. We Americans think of ourselves as educated and sophisticated, but the sheer difficulty of finding the root causes of phenomena makes it easy for anyone to go wrong in this way. That basic cognitive problem can be exacerbated by politicians with agendas that are sometimes hidden and sometimes blatantly obvious.

What does this have to do with business? Simply put, every organization has problems. But if you want to fix a problem, the solution must be on target. As an example, I have seen people get fired because of problems, only for it to emerge later that the problems persist, proving that these people were not the true source of these problems. This is a common, and quite evil, "error" made by managers who are "blamers." And the conflation of unrelated phenomena can go on and on, particularly if the leadership is too stupid or too arrogant or too lazy to figure out what is really going on.

There are two key errors that can occur in defining a problem. The first is defining a problem in such a way that the solution is implied. The second is accepting at face value the assumptions about causation in the way the problem is defined. See Eugene Bardach and Eric

M. Patashnik, *A Practical Guide for Policy Analysis* (Sage, 2016, fifth edition), page 11. An example is a legislative proposal for physician-assisted suicide. Query: Why do we put physicians at the center of that, when many of them don't want to be there? By putting them in the title, we make an assumption that isn't warranted and foreclose other options too quickly. Also note that a "problem" is to some extent in the eye of the beholder and depends partly on expectations and ideology. What my boss sees as a problem, I might see as the ordinary state of affairs. I remember asking my secretary as a first-year lawyer to delete a prior document draft from her computer. She asked me: "Why, is it bothering you?" Good question.

We must recognize not only that some problems can't be solved but that hammering away blindly at a problem can be counterproductive, even if it is ultimately solvable. I picked up a nice brochure from my church called "Strengthening a Struggling Marriage" by Louisa Rogers. She says, quite brilliantly, at one point, that "sometimes a problem benefits from benign neglect; with a little distance, it may fade in importance and urgency." That is not just an idea for marriages; it is also an idea for running a business (or government agency). Now, obviously it can't be used in all situations because some problems can destroy you if they aren't confronted in a timely way. But simply being a busybody about solving problems isn't always good either, and that's the point. Doesn't it matter whether the persons intervening know what they're doing? Doesn't it matter how the intervention is designed? If you're going to intervene, try to avoid making the situation worse.

Another way of expressing the idea that we don't want to misattribute causation is simply to say that we want to identify and define problems correctly.

CHAPTER **12**
Leadership

I have written about leadership before in my books *Basic Stuff That Everyone Should Know* and *No More Stupidtry: Insights for the Modern World*. I have read many books on leadership; in fact, I read my first leadership book in the ninth grade when I was class president. The problem with a lot of these books is that you tend to forget what's in them soon after you read them. That's because they are just too darn complicated. For example, a given book might list twenty attributes of a leader. How can anyone hold all of that in their heads?

I boil leadership down to *trust* and *credibility*. While the *goal* of leadership is to get people to work together, trust and credibility are the *means* by which you make it happen. Your employees do not have a right to expect you as their leader to share their moral, social, and political values or viewpoints. But they do have a right to expect that you will not lie to them and that you will not break the law. Also, if you don't know your stuff, eventually your employees will leave because they know that an incompetent leader is a danger not only to himself but to others.

Actually, I can boil trust and credibility down to something even simpler: *authenticity*. It takes confidence to be yourself—not the confidence of one who lives off his or her surface appearance but of one who has something inside them, a core that exists independently of the applause of others. Just wanting to be liked can often lead to the opposite result if it distorts your decision-making or makes you seem fake. It's not necessary for people to agree with you all the time or like everything about you. If you're real, then there is a foundation upon which trust can be built.

As Michael Douglas says in the movie *The American President*, "I can tell you that leadership is all about character." Everyone is selfish to some extent, but a leader must show that he or she can think about others and show some consideration. The first reason is that if your employees get the idea that you will throw them under the bus at the first sign of trouble, they'll leave. Loyalty isn't something automatically owed to a supervisor by virtue of their position; it must be earned. The second reason is that doing selfish things like blaming your staff is demotivating. If things go wrong and you are the leader, you need to be honest about the fact that there is some aspect of you that is partly to blame for that.

In addition, if you can stow your ego and not insist on taking credit for everything good that happens or on proving that you're always right about everything, it will smooth things out. It is smoother to let people think they came up with the idea that you put in their heads instead of insisting that it was your idea. As Harry Truman famously said: "You can accomplish anything in life, provided that you do not mind who gets the credit"—quoted by Jim Collins, *Good to Great: Why Some Companies Make the Leap ... and Others Don't* (HarperCollins, 2001), page 17. Insecurity can be a great motivator, but in a leader, it tends to result in dysfunctional behavior.

No leader should assume that all solutions will come from their own head. Solutions may come from any part of the organization or from outside the organization. A leader provides guidance and inspiration, but should not expect to be a demi-God.

A good leader should be a good listener. One of our presidents famously told one of his staffers "If you're so smart, then why aren't you President?" Now, I understand the temptation to put an empty suit from an overrated school in his place, but that message shows extremely poor leadership skills. It takes a true egoist to think that he doesn't need to hear the advice of others, and pulling rank reveals insecurity.

Employees need a leader to be more than just a friend in the same way that children need their parents to be more than just friends. There is a role-playing aspect to leadership, and therefore not all of it can come naturally. And remember that you lead with your personality, not your position. Your position is an inanimate object like a chair. Asking people to respect your position and the power vested in it is like asking them to respect a sofa. Leading is more than just being a boss or a manager.

More and more we are recognizing that some people in an organization lead from positions other than the top. People who use their job title to lead are using a crutch.

Ask yourself, what are you leading? You are leading a *team*, not a bunch of independent people. The trick is that each of the people on that team is different and won't respond in the same way to the things you do. For example, some people do well in an unstructured environment, while others need both structure and direction; some people like compliments, and others resent them. That doesn't mean that you have to be a chameleon. It just means that you have to be aware that one size does not fit all. To editorialize a bit, one challenge with having both men and women in an office is the danger that women's desire for politeness and decorum adversely affects the aggressiveness that some men are capable of and which is sometimes needed. Another challenge is having women or minorities believe that there is a level enough playing field with men that they can afford to play fair.

Remember this admonition from Scripture: "Thou hypocrite, first cast the beam out of thine own eye; and then shalt thou see clearly to cast out the mote out of thy brother's eye" (Matthew 7:5). A more modern formulation comes from David Peter Stroh's book *Systems Thinking and Social Change* (Charles Green Publishing, 2015), pages 22–23:

> The simple fact is that most managers do not *experience* that they are contributing to creating their current reality. So they don't see how they can

contribute to changing that reality. When people fail to see their responsibility for the present, they (1) tend to assume that their primary work is to change others or the system—not themselves, and (2) promote solutions that optimize their part of the system based on a mistaken belief that the way to optimize the whole system is to optimize each of the parts. By contrast, a systems view encourages them to critically assess their own contributions first.

In other words: Physician, heal thyself, and Charity begins at home. Let me put it another way: There is a difference between tinkering with *things* and tinkering with *people*.

In addition, although this is arguably more management theory than leadership theory, there is no way to do a one-size-fits-all delegation style or a one-size-fits-all control freak style. It depends on the person, the task to be performed, and the situation. But recognize that even if you delegate, you still must monitor what is going on, and that if you delegate to someone who is completely goofy, it is going to raise a question about your judgment. Consider the distinction between competence and control. Some people hire for control instead of competence and this often results in dysfunction. It can be nice to be all powerful, but you better be darn smart and knowledgeable, and pretty much everyone will fail this criteria.

What about "automated" management like pay-for-performance schemes or computer tracking of documents with tickler systems? There is a role for these, but if you spot a manager who is using them as a crutch to avoid personal engagement with other people, with all the emotions and conflict and chaos that go along with it, just be careful: over time things can really go south under someone like that. Management is always partly about being a people person. Whether one is basically an introvert or an extrovert is beside the point. Note that the decision whether to use a phone, an e-mail, a letter, a meeting in your office, or a walk past someone else's workstation is an important decision. Merely defaulting to e-mail for everything is a mistake because it is not at all appropriate for some conversations.

I will be the first to admit that there is not enough in this book about how to make change in a complex organization operating in a dynamic environment. Why not? There isn't a cookbook for that, really. CEOs in the United States get paid more than in Europe, which I'm not sure makes total sense, and I do think that boards of directors are bit at the mercy of an elite group who are hanging them out to dry. However, a great CEO can add tremendous value if change is needed. You have to see the future and know how to make change, and in truth not many people can do that. No one has a crystal ball. A big ship doesn't turn on a dime. At a minimum, however, good management requires giving staff a head's up so they can anticipate and have time to react and plan. Not everyone has an equal ability to see the road ahead, but a leader needs to do better than most to succeed.

My own personal view is that a great leader must be part lifetime learner and part lifetime teacher—and in that regard (among others), please notice that the leader is a vendor of services to his staff, not someone ordering people about. And to elaborate on the point about being a teacher: there are many different teaching styles, but good teachers will encourage their students, not belittle them. Some teachers are scarier than others, but there is a big difference between being scary and being mean. I think people, from the time they are children, know when someone is trying to help them and when someone is trying to mess them up. You just get that feeling about people.

Now, you may ask yourself: "Why should I listen to this author or any academic or consultant?" Good question. How about listening to someone who got super-rich by being super-clever in delivering products and services to the public? Sam Walton of Wal-Mart put it this way:

"Outstanding leaders go out of their way to boost the self-esteem of their personnel. If people believe in themselves, it's amazing what they can accomplish."

CHAPTER 13

Psychology

Psychology has always struggled to prove that it is a science. It isn't, although with more knowledge about brain chemistry and hard-wiring, it may become more of a science as time passes. We still know relatively little about the brain. That said, I am fond of Ivan Pavlov, B F Skinner, and Alfred Adler because I think operant conditioning and birth order theories are based on solid fact. I also find value in modern thinking about cognitive biases, such as observation bias (limitations of point of view), recall bias (limitations of memory), and confirmation bias (preferring facts that confirm preconceptions). I have observed many people engage in cherry-picking facts, making decisions first and then looking for facts to justify themselves on a post-hoc basis. In fact, I have seen managers go after staff they don't like by looking for things to make an issue out of. No one is perfect, so that is a possible course of action, but it is not fair and it does not inspire confidence.

The theory of retrograde falsification says that sometimes people will write over old memories so that what they remember didn't really ever happen. It is also important to know about projection, which means that people sometimes attribute their own ideas, feelings, and attitudes to other people. As we said as kids: "I know you are, but what am I?" See, even children know this stuff without being told by some PhD. A specific manifestation of this that is very dangerous is when management is messing things up and they project their own flaws onto their staff and deflect by blaming the staff. People in leadership often have big egos, and they have a powerful psychological need to deny their own failures and to minimize the abilities and achievements of others. Watch out for that one; it is as common as the day is long. One of the many great lines from the movie *Jaws* is when Quint, played by Robert Shaw, is scolding Hooper, played by Richard Dreyfuss. He says: "Well, it proves one thing, Mr. Hooper. It proves that you wealthy college boys don't have the education enough to admit when you're wrong." I wish more people would take that lesson and not allow their need to protect their fragile egos to force them further and further into delusion.

An important point from operant conditioning is that punishment sometimes ingrains the bad behavior. That is why positive reinforcement can sometimes be helpful. Carrots more than sticks, although you normally need both.

One of Alfred Adler's contributions was the idea of an "inferiority complex." My own view is that a little sense of inferiority can help spur one toward greater achievement, but if the sense of inferiority runs deep enough, it can cause a person to go around putting people down and hurting others in order to prove their own power and superiority. Of course, this idea goes back a lot farther than Alfred Alder. Try reading Shakespeare's play *The Tragedy of King Richard the Third*, which is about a deformed man who becomes a king and a supervillain. Richard III says this about himself in his opening soliloquy:

> But I, that am not shaped for sportive tricks
> Nor made to court an amorous looking glass;
> I, that am rudely stamped and want love's majesty
> To strut before a wanton ambling nymph ....

Simply put, Richard doesn't get to bed the pretty girls, and that's why he's a major jerk. Simple, but sometimes the truth is simple, or as one of my literature professors said: "The truth is superficial." Now, most people don't have serious physical challenges—the scars they carry are inside their psyches. Some people look fine on the outside, but they think of themselves as ugly. Note also that sometimes young people, women, and minorities can feel powerless or inferior and that this sense of victimhood can create unhelpful behavior. Try to be understanding and work toward a solution. True confidence sometimes takes a lifetime to build.

Another aspect of modern psychology is the realization that a person's psychological state at any given moment is partly a function of the situation they find themselves in. Now, that doesn't mean that we don't hold people accountable for their actions. But it does mean that we should always consider things in context. Behavior is not only about character. Given bad enough circumstances, even good-natured people can do very bad things.

Another key finding from psychology is that the human mind tends to oversimplify its view of the world into rules for thinking (called "heuristics") and even stereotypes. The reason is that it is not efficient to do complete analysis on everything—one must size up a situation quickly in order to survive. But these shortcuts are not the same thing as careful scientific analysis or due-diligence research, and we must always be mindful that we are sometimes oversimplifying.

Nobody's perfect. Each of your employees will be a mixed bag, just as you are. So you have to take the good with the bad. Expecting perfection is not rational, unless you see yourself as superior the way that some people with power mistakenly do. In the old days we called these people idolaters, because they worship themselves, and they do not give credit to God for the good things that happen in their lives. Not to proselytize, but for my own part I think of God as a jealous God, and I try to show some humility so that bad things don't happen to me. We Christians like to frame our own achievements as being for the greater glory of God, not for the greater glory of ourselves. Anyway, that's our goal.

A word about compensation policy. If you pay people a lot, they may become swelled-headed and think they're smarter than they are. That arrogance can become a problem if you don't find a way to address it. Pretentious titles can have a similar effect. That's why you want to hire real people who have their feet on the ground. Effective employees must know what they don't know.

How do you know when someone is suffering from undue arrogance? They play power games, they act vindictively or arbitrarily, they overemphasize their own opinions and approaches, they isolate themselves by using their minions as a buffer, they stop trying to justify their actions with logic and start lying about their motives, they subvert orderly (and sometimes even lawful) process to achieve the results they want, they see themselves as indispensable to the organization, and they start promoting based on sycophancy instead of merit. As Lord Acton put it: "Power tends to corrupt, and absolute power corrupts absolutely." Some chalk it up to insecurity and an oversized ego. See, e.g., John C. Maxwell, *What Successful People Know about Leadership* (Center Street, 2016), pages 3–5. Others view it in a religious context. As Gary V. Smith points out in his analysis of Scripture:

> Once people begin to amass expensive homes, power over other people, and a big income, it is easy for them to find their identity and value in these things. If a person's reputation and hope for the future is invested in these material values, there is a natural tendency to place one's security in them. When possessions take on this kind of importance, people will go to great extremes to protect their own power. Moreover, when anything seriously threatens their status, they

will sometimes act in illegal or immoral ways to maintain their affluent lifestyle. Amos views these as false sources of security that God will remove. (*The NIV Application Commentary: Hosea, Amos, Micah* [Zondervan, 2001], page 290)

John Steinbeck did a riff on Lord Acton's law: "Power does not corrupt. Fear corrupts ... Perhaps a fear of the loss of power." My own view is that some people don't have a life outside of work, and that forces them to accord their work and the identity it provides them with undue importance. For example, I play the piano, and I listen to music. No boss can take that away from me. I carry that inside myself regardless of what job I have.

Every now and then a manager has to deal with a problem employee who manifests psychological issues. Sometimes these issues have a basis in brain chemistry or deep-seated emotional damage from early childhood. That is hard for a manager to fix. But at other times people's psychological problems are primarily due to their inability to think about anything other than themselves. Just remind them of the big world out there with lots of people just like them and lots of problems to solve. When I meet people who talk a lot about themselves, I know I have a potential problem on my hands. Also, beware of people who thrive on chaos and conflict. They might be unconsciously creating problems just because they wish to recreate the dysfunction of their childhood environment.

Now let's tie this chapter on psychology back to the chapter on misattribution of causation. What is at issue in misreading a given text, person, or situation is that every human being in engaged in a continual process of interpretation, attempting to make sense of and derive meaning from what is before them. There is an important academic area on this subject called hermeneutics which represents the culmination of several disciplines including philosophy and literary criticism. A good explanation of the basics follows:

> Hermeneutic thinkers argue that understanding is the interpretive act of integrating particular things such as words, signs, and events into a meaningful whole. We understand an object, word, or fact when it makes sense within our own life context and thus speaks to us meaningfully. When we understand objects, texts, or situations in this way, they become part of our inner mental world so that we can express them again in our own terms. (Jens Zimmermann, *Hermeneutics: A Very Short Introduction* [Oxford, 2015], page 7)

What is the takeaway on hermeneutics? Simply that we are subjective creatures and we must recognize this limitation in ourselves. Brilliant insight, right? But guess what: this wisdom is ancient. It goes back at least to the Romans. As Marcus Aurelius wrote: "Consider that everything is opinion, and opinion is in your power" (*Meditations* [Dover, 1997], page 96 [book XII]). FYI: he attributes this idea that "all is opinion" to the Cynic Monimus (page

11 [book II]). Christians or adherents of Confucianism would simply say that we should exhibit humility.

Some of the best businesspeople I have met didn't think they were good at it. It wasn't false modesty; it was simply that every day they were testing themselves against the rigor of the marketplace. Conversely, people with giant egos are usually idiots. My first boss said it well: "If you start thinking you're good, then you're gonna go downhill." Tom Nichols, who has written on the backlash against experts, observes that

> The least competent people turn out to be the ones least likely to realize they are wrong and others are right, the most likely to respond to their own ignorance by trying to fake it, and the least able to learn anything. ("How Americans Lost Faith in Expertise," *Foreign Affairs* [March/April 2017], page 66)

In the simplest terms, humility is a sign of perspective, which is sometimes a sign of intelligence. I am fortunate to be well read in the history of ideas and I can boil down the last few thousand years of a big part of that development to a single conclusion: the human mind is imperfect, and our knowledge is uncertain, in part because the mind is separate from the external world, and there is no real or physical connection between our words and the things that they point to. Of course we should know that already without even reading one philosophy book. My point is that a lot of spadework has been done on the issue, and it has been confirmed (surprise, surprise) that we're just not that smart. Of course the other major thrust of Western philosophy is to reinforce the idea that doing things that benefit people other than yourself is important.

Psychology is related to marketing, obviously, and in a larger sense to markets generally. The behavior of buyers and sellers is about psychology, as is the use of incentives to modify that behavior. This is why a good businessperson is part "demon neurologist." My father was a businessman, but he started out as a probation officer, and his college degree was in sociology, so he had an understanding of people. I think that helped him in business. IT entrepreneur Alex Becker put it well:

> Many people fail to understand this when they start a business, and they therefore try to forge a business without thinking about people. They forget that they must lead people. They forget that they must persuade people. They forget that they must influence people first and foremost. They forget that they must have something that makes people want to give them money. (*The 10 Pillars of Wealth: Mind-Sets of the World's Richest People* [Brown Books, 2016], page 139)

When those of us experienced in implementation say something isn't going to work, we are usually not talking about technology. What we are usually saying is "People won't do that."

14

Communications and Marketing

Communications are partly about what you intend, partly about what you say, and partly about what people hear and those are not always the same thing. You get out of things what you bring to them. With any communications you have to know your target audience (or in business-speak, your "target market"). Marketers also talk about segmentation, but I'm not sure this is anything more than analyzing the target market in detail. One should also consider the fact that people outside the target may hear your message, and their reactions might matter to some extent.

What is the number-one cardinal rule of communications? Let the other person finish his or her sentence, absent a good reason not to. Why? Because you cannot read people's minds, and you do not know what they are going to say until they say it. So it is better not to rush to conclusions about where they are going, start to talk, and say foolish things that are nonresponsive, irrelevant, and just plain wrong. Calm yourself. No need to appear impetuous and immature. As the old saying goes, you will learn more by listening than by talking. And of course, you don't want to embarrass your parents, dead or alive, by making it look like they weren't paying any attention when you were a kid.

When evaluating your marketing "argument," you have to be like a lawyer, only better. When I first started talking about my book *No More Stupidtry: Insights for the Modern World* (2016), I made an economic development argument. That makes sense, but it is true of any type of education, so it doesn't differentiate my book from other books or teaching approaches. Similarly, remember when John Kerry ran for president, and he started his convention by saluting and saying, "John Kerry, reporting for duty." If being a war veteran means that you should be president, then we have many prospects to choose from. That argument is too broad and is a bit illogical, so how can it be very effective?

When I started out in management, I missed a letter from a government regulator. One my board members who was a big-time bank CEO said, "A missed communication like that is not acceptable." I agree. Any serious communication that calls for a response should be responded to, although as a lawyer, I can tell you that does not mean that every question should be answered. There is something rude about not responding to a communication. It is like sending a message that the person trying to communicate is inferior. Of course we do that on purpose sometimes, but generally it isn't a good idea to make someone feel unimportant. In addition, observe that just the fact that a question must be answered doesn't resolve the question of who should answer it. Notice also that I have classified some communications as not requiring a response. What do I mean? For example, I have some very smart contacts, and I like to talk at them, show them my comments on this or that issue, but I don't get a response 96 percent of the time. Why not? Because I'm merely offering thoughts for what they're worth—for consideration on the other end. It helps me learn if I get a response, and that's what I hope for, but I don't expect it. People don't always want to opine publicly on every subject.

With any communication, but particularly with a written communication, you need to assume that the communication can fall into the wrong hands and write for the variety of audiences that may see it, including a jury. Also, while I believe strongly in authenticity, one should be mindful of whether a communication makes one look bigger or smaller. It may be authentic to lash out at someone when you get angry, but sometimes it is better to stay above the fray. People have egos and need their dignity respected.

Marketing is a complicated field, and there is a psychological and sociological aspect to it. When making an argument, just make sure that the listener gives a hoot about it, because not everyone is similarly situated. Print and television advertising normally has to be very simple and limited to creating brand awareness or brand image. Complicated messaging (like consumer education) usually doesn't work, unless it is a message that the audience already knows, like "Tobacco kills." If you think about the various types of media and their limited reach and the fact that people are being bombarded by thousands of messages per day, you will see that marketing your business isn't going to be easy or quick. But obviously if no one knows about you, you aren't going to sell anything.

Price is part of marketing because some people associate higher price with higher quality. Why do some people pay $1,000 for a designer Italian bag when they can get a knockoff for $25? It's psychological. If you want to signal your wealth to others the way a peacock shows off its feathers, then you need overpriced stuff. This point is important because income inequality is growing, and when the economy goes bad, the first people to lose purchasing power are the working and middle classes. The high-end market will always be there.

That said, not everyone is enamored of a high price. Many people, and I am one of them, are value purchasers. For example, I was always happy to buy a compact disc of a very good classical music performance because if I paid $15 and listened to the item 200 times, the per-hearing cost was less than eight cents. I consider that an intelligent expenditure of money. In addition, I will pay a high price if I am getting high value. The founder of the Oreck vacuum manufacturing firm put it well: "Effective marketing is about value, not about price; yet messing with price can have devastating effects on the bottom line which makes me wonder why businesses do it all the time" (David Oreck, *From Dust to Diamonds: How Small*

Entrepreneurs Can Grow and Prosper in Any Economy [TAG, 2013], page 20).

I have a good marketing story from the political arena. Midway through Mitt Romney's presidential bid against President Obama, I wrote to the campaign manager and told him that they didn't have a message. They sent me back a dozen position papers on various policy issues. That's perhaps what you might expect from a campaign that has a fifty-point plan to improve America on its website. Romney might have been a fine consultant and finance expert, but he knew nothing about marketing. He was interviewed and asked, "Why do you want to be president?" He said: "Because I love this country." Really? Well, since Mitt is the only one, I guess it makes sense that out of about 320 million people, he should be the only one to be president. The Romney team simply didn't get it. They didn't have a message. Before you market, you have to figure yourself out.

A word about sales. I think pushy salesmen are bad salesmen. The best salesmen (and the best lobbyists) I know seek only to be a credible source of information. That's how you foster trust. In addition, a good salesman is sometimes willing to do added-value service on an uncompensated basis—in other words, favors. Clients like vendors who visibly want to help them.

One must observe that there is a difference between marketing and consumer education. Marketing is generally used for creating awareness that a product exists or burnishing a brand. But sometimes those efforts are futile without people that have enough understanding and background to act. For example, one can do marketing on the existence of a local symphony orchestra, but it takes a lot of consumer education to persuade people who are not already lovers of classical music why they should shell out so much money to listen to music by composers who died before they were born. The learning curve for classical music can be steep.

In politics, they talk about message discipline or more simply "staying on message." That means that one has to understand that messages can get lost if listeners are pulled into too many unimportant matters that are not central to the objective. Of course, one has to formulate the message correctly in the first place. When the Affordable Care Act was rolled out, the Democrats called it "health reform," which scared people. They should have called it reform of "health insurance" or "health finance." That rather careless error created unnecessary opposition and confusion from the start.

To run the risk of restating the obvious, in order to sell to a prospect, you will need information about the prospect. There are different ways and times to gather this kind of information, but if you don't have all the key facts about the customer's needs, you might not fashion the right solution or explain your offering the right way. That doesn't mean that you have to be made of Play-Doh and bend all over the place—and you shouldn't, because if clients don't respect you, they won't follow your lead. It just means that you have to know who you're talking to.

I want to talk about my favorite television commercial. It was done for DeBeers diamonds. It was a short, silent movie of a young couple walking down a path in a wooded park. Ahead of them is an elderly couple. They separate to pass on either side of the elderly couple and continue walking ahead of them. Then they look back at them and then at each other. What the producers of that commercial realized is that the value of a diamond is not that it is shiny and expensive. The producers knew that the true value of a diamond is that it is a symbol that means "forever." Beautiful message, and it could not have been simpler. The entire commercial is designed to burnish DeBeers' brand image. Do you know that (at least when I knew a student there) the first assignment at NYU film school is a silent film? That's the question: can you tell a story without words? That is film in its purest form. The lesson is simply that you have to understand the medium that you are using because they don't all work the same way.

Finally, what if something happens in your company that could lead to a lawsuit or a public relations problem? First thing: don't panic. Don't issue a premature communication on the incident. First issue a placeholder communication to the effect that you are gathering information about the incident to hear from all sides and will comment soon. Then find the facts, and talk to all of the relevant advisers and someone who actually cares about you as a person, and formulate a response.

We now live in a twenty-four-hour news cycle, and there is pressure for speed of communication, but resist such pressure, because once a communication is out the door, if you try to walk it back later, you just end up looking disingenuous. If some adversarial lawyers and media types push you into doing the right thing, you don't look as good as if you do the right thing up front. Moreover, in a world where every smartphone has a video camera, it is not just a question of being legally in the right, it is a question of optics, perception, and the emotional responses of the public.

Now, what if your staff has done something clearly wrong and outside the lines? Do you defend them and circle the wagons? Complicated questions. It depends. Just remember the song that said that "fools rush in" or the old saying that you should "look before you leap."

CHAPTER 15

CHAPTER
Negotiations

Most negotiations are not about clever argumentation but about power and who needs whom more. As a bond lawyer told me: "You know the Golden Rule? He who has the gold makes the rules." That is, money talks. Also, if you can walk away, then you have power. In fact the vast majority of business transactions are not negotiated at all. We just use a form contract, what lawyers call a "contract of adhesion." The buyer just signs on the dotted line. This is good because it reduces transaction costs, but it can force buyers into agreements that aren't favorable to them. The only saving grace is that ambiguities in a contract of adhesion are construed against the party responsible for drafting the contract.

The other big issue in negotiations is time. If you have more time and can wait longer than your opponent, you have leverage.

Here's the big question: does bluffing work? To me, it doesn't if the relative bargaining power of the parties is clear. You can only really bluff if you may actually carry out your threat. But I guess it depends in part on the kind of person you are. The thing is that if you push too hard and overplay your hand when it is obvious that you have no negotiating position, your opponents may see it as an insult to their intelligence.

A few basic principles are applicable to negotiations. You need to be a good listener. You don't want to give away the whole store up front, you want to hold things back for later horse-trading. You should estimate what your opponent's end is (i.e., what is he making off the deal) as closely as you can. Deals should be win–win, to the extent possible, so don't think that it is a bad thing if your opponent makes a little money. After all, you don't want to get a reputation for being a skinflint because in the long run it can hurt you. People do business with other people in order to make money. If you're constantly screwing people over, people will try to avoid you. In other words, if you leave something on the table, don't fret unduly about it. My philosophy is that people who work for a living need incentives to keep doing so, and if I have to pay a little extra here and there to maintain those incentives, I don't mind. I don't think there is any such thing as "trickle-down" economics, but if you believe in that, then you better do some trickling.

In particular, try to avoid doing things that will leave a bug permanently running around in your opponent's head. True hatred isn't built in a day. It starts from a small, hard nugget of something that grows and grows as layers of resentment build on top of it over the passage of years. The ideal result for any deal is that after it is done, it is forgotten by both parties. A fair deal is a forgotten deal. When you get rooked, you never forget it. In my last book

I said that if you take care of your vendors, they'll take care of you. True, some vendors are fraudsters and jerks, and anyway no one can afford to be Santa Claus all the time. But still, that saying is often true.

Perhaps a concrete example from real life will help illustrate what can go wrong in a negotiation. When I went to law school, one of the first things I did was go looking for a used upright piano. I went to this music store, and the lady asked me what price range I was looking for. So I said five hundred dollars. And she waved her hand at all the pianos and said: "These are all five hundred dollars." Duh, just fell off the turnip truck, huh? Call me Goober Lim.

Dealing with the Law and Lawyers

I have discussed this topic in two prior books, so I want to be relatively brief. Legal reasoning involves that navigation between the law, stated in words, and the facts of the particular case. You can read a rule with ease, but you cannot know how it operates on a set of facts to produce a legal conclusion until you know those facts. Who is in control of those facts? Often you are, as the business manager or owner. It's your fact pattern; take responsibility for it, and don't blame the lawyer.

The nature of legal reasoning means that the legal conclusion or answer is not always completely clear. And remember, that what you are looking for is not a clever argument. You are looking for a winning argument. Play to win. Don't play to lose and enrich lawyers who don't care much whether you live or die. If lawyers are billing hours (not going on contingency), then they enrich themselves whether you win or lose. Clever, no?

In addition, when doing legal compliance, you should take the time to create an outline/summary of the applicable statutes so that you can find your own way through them, even if you are working with a lawyer. The reason is that you need to know enough to spot legal issues for transmittal to your lawyer because lawyers are typically trapped in their law firm and haven't got a clue what is going on in your business until you tell them. You don't have to know enough law to find the right answers, but you have to know enough law to ask the right questions. It is easy to get angry at a legislature for writing goofy statutes, but if you ask yourself what rationale they might have had for doing what they did, it may make your compliance tasks easier to bear.

One bit of law trivia that is useful to know is that not all contracts have to be in writing. Sometimes oral contracts can be enforced. Indeed, under the doctrines of promissory estoppel or detrimental reliance, you might even get stuck with a promise even though a true contract was never formed. So try to act ethically when dealing with people, and avoid pulling the old bait and switch. The contract is there for the day you end up in litigation, so remember that they key is to do business with the right people. If you do that, hopefully the contract will be irrelevant.

Law can be bewildering, so it helps to step back and think simply about it. If you go to court, you're going to have to tell a story and it had better make sense and not have a lot of holes in it. You're going to say this, and the other side is going to say that, and then you're going to say something in response. You're going to get asked questions and you had better have answers. So think through the debate in advance.

For example, let's say that you were going to tell a story about how O.J. Simpson deserved the death penalty for his "cold-blooded premeditation," but you wondered how to explain the fact that Ron Goldman just happened to be walking up the path to Nicole Brown Simpson's house in an attempt to return her sunglasses at the precise moment when the premediated act was occurring. Or let's say that you were going to tell a story about how Casey Anthony deserved the death penalty because she murdered her little girl Caylee, even though you have no idea how the child died because by the time the body was found all the soft tissue was gone and the site was altered by the weather. As I said before, we don't blame lawyers for the facts, but we do blame them if they don't understand the strengths and weaknesses of their case.

What's the other key thing to remember about the law? Remember the line from the movie "A Few Good Men" when Tom Cruise (as Kaffee) is ragging on Demi Moore (as Galloway)? He says: "I keep forgetting that you were absent the day they taught law at law school. It's not about what I believe, it's about what I can prove." There are complicated aspects to proving things, including but not limited to the rules of evidence and certain exclusionary rules associated with the U.S. Constitution. Just because it's in your head, doesn't mean that it's going to end up in front of the judge or jury.

If you get sued for negligence, then by definition the outcome of your work was bad, but your liability depends on whether your procedures were reasonable and in keeping with whatever duty of care is applicable. In other words, the benefit of having defined procedures is that sometimes you can use them as a defense in a lawsuit.

Colloquially, we say "no harm, no foul." Generally, in civil litigation that is true. People aren't going to sue you unless they can get money, and there must be some showing of damage. But business regulation isn't always written that way. You can get in trouble with regulators even if there isn't any evidence that anyone was harmed.

In addition to tort negligence cases and business regulation, you need to be aware of other legal doctrines in the commercial area such as the implied warranty of merchantability, the implied warranty of fitness for a particular purpose, and the Uniform Commercial Code (UCC) which governs many commercial transactions.

Lawyers are expensive, but when starting something, they can play an important role. For example, if one writes documentation for real estate the wrong way, and the problem goes undetected for a long time, the consequences can be severe. A good lawyer isn't just someone who sues people. A good lawyer is someone who tries to manage every client's risk down to a reasonable level. Avoidance of lawsuits trumps litigation.

Bear in mind that lawyers are busy, and they are not mind-readers, so if you have a pressing deadline, you need to explain the circumstances fully. You cannot just say, "ASAP." Also, and this is critical, when corporate documents are being prepared (as opposed to litigation), you have to read what the lawyer produces very carefully. You cannot ever assume that any lawyer can be trusted to just take care of it on a fully delegated basis. Think of corporate legal work as a team effort.

Most people use language to convey ideas, but lawyers often use language to achieve a concrete result, what we might call "operative" language. In other words, for lawyers, language is sometimes action. If there are "magic words" that you don't understand, you have a right to ask what the meaning and consequences of those words are, because it is easy for lawyers to make it look like they are meeting your need when in reality they are not getting all the way there.

Tell your employees that e-mail is part of the public record and is normally discoverable in litigation. Off-color jokes and romantic chitchat are best left to oral communication. Tell your employees that when they write a letter, they need to put a date on it. Tell your managers that no letter should go out from your firm that does not have a return address or contact information of some kind. In a sane world I wouldn't have to say these things, but my comments are based on actual experience with real companies of today.

About 80 percent of lawsuits settle before trial, so please don't think of going to trial as an opportunity to vindicate yourself. When you go to court, you roll the dice. In fact, the better case you have, the easier it should be to get your opponent to settle. Almost by definition, if a case is in court, it is most often because it is a difficult, close case that could go either way. Pick your battles, if you can.

Some of you will remember that in Charles Dickens's novel *Oliver Twist* there is a character named Mr. Bumble who says, "The law is a ass—a idiot." Why might that be true, at least some of the time? The making of laws is a human endeavor, and it is not as easy as it looks, but more important, no written rule can ever capture all the nuances of every single factual situation or case that might arise. When the facts do not fit what the legislators had in mind when they wrote the law, you can have adverse consequences. Law isn't perfect, but that doesn't mean that we can do without it.

A quick look back into history might be helpful. In some areas, law has become Byzantine in its complexity, and this has created problems and fostered opposition. But not all laws are of recent inception. We can find the origins of our contract law, tort law, criminal law, and property law in the Roman Empire.

There have been two major paradigm shifts since then. First, in those days peace meant order through repression by government power. Today, we have learned that people like freedom, and they can be more easily reconciled to their situation if we don't try to control them too much. Second, in those days there wasn't always a clear distinction between the government and religion. Today, we in the West try to maintain that separation, partly to avoid religious persecution and excessive government interference in daily life, but also because it helps the market system flourish.

What's the point that I am trying to make? Even though some of us think the government and the lawyers have gotten out of control, we don't want to throw the baby out with the bathwater. Some of this law stuff is necessary to run a society and an economy.

Finally, a wise word from Benjamin Franklin: "Tricks and Treachery are the Practice of Fools, that have not Wit enough to be honest." In the United States, the wheels of justice turn very slowly, such that one might think that one is getting away with something. Some do, but the bigger the infraction, the more likely the eventual punishment. To the person who gets caught in the machinery of justice, the experience is typically drawn out, unpleasant and expensive (to say nothing of inconsistent as to outcomes). Put it on your list of things to avoid.

CHAPTER 17

Dealing with the Government

Someone once told me that the business position on government policy is often neutrality. I go a step further. As a businessperson I try to stay entirely away from the government. I don't want to attract the attention of the government, so I steer clear. I pay my taxes and license fees and try to keep myself in compliance with law. That's all. It is true that some businesses can make huge money as government vendors, but to me it is like getting in bed with Satan. When I worked in securities law compliance, I dealt with the SEC. My boss would say, "Put on your kneepads, and talk to them." In other words, grovel before the tin god that is the government bureaucrat. I'm sad to report that some bureaucrats have inferiority complexes, and they compensate by pushing people around. When I worked in the government, I tried to avoid being that kind of person, and I was not alone. But if you try to be high-handed with some bureaucrats, the long-term consequences can be negative. At the very least, you can be made to wait a long time.

If you write a letter to a government agency, keep it short, and stick to the facts. And don't waste people's time unless the topic really matters to you. In the law, we have an objection if a lawyer keeps badgering the witness for the same information. We say "asked and answered." Most government people won't answer a policy or legal question unless prior thought went into it. So while giving up isn't necessarily good, at some point one needs to know when one is beating a dead horse. Asked and answered.

When talking to policymakers about business regulation, don't come out completely against the whole idea of it. Not all regulation is bad. Why do we have regulations (i.e., laws)? To stop one party from harming another party. Is that really something you want to come out publicly against? So don't say that the government shouldn't tell businesspeople what to do. Just say that you don't want government regulation to micromanage or over-specify or go into areas of minor or indirect harm. That kind of statement is reasonable and difficult to argue with. Most experienced legislators and other government operatives know that if they overreach, there will be blowback. If legislators are about to enact a law that is not going to work and will blow back in their faces later, they probably would like to know that up front, so please speak up if no one else is doing so. The hardest thing in legislating is to make sure that the reality underlying the legislation is fully understood.

It is never "all government" or "all market"; there is always a carefully calibrated balance to be struck between the two. If the economy is bad, blaming the government is sometimes right but not always. North Korea has too much government for a robust economy, and Afghanistan has too little. There is a balance to be struck. The idea of bigger government is like salt in the cooking—it makes things better until it doesn't. Balance, moderation, the golden mean between two extremes, and "Goldilocks and the Three Bears"—one chair was "just right."

Note that government has distinct roles as a provider of market infrastructure, as a regulator of behavior, and as a market participant. Generally, it is better if the government provides a level playing field than if it engages in crony capitalism, but to achieve that goal, private business must be willing to restrain its natural desire to obtain special government franchises and protections. How about the famed public-private partnership? The success of any given public-private partnership will depend on exactly how it is designed and run (and for how long).

The biggest problem with government regulation is that the law almost always means a "one size fits all" approach, which is inflexible because law is hard to change. Where does government work best? With USC—not University of Southern California or even U.S. Code, but where *uniformity, stability, and continuity* are required. If change, adaptation, flexibility and innovation are required, the government can be clumsy. All that said, while I have often made the point that complex business regulations favor large businesses over small, not all industries have a lot of small businesses. Don't expect to see Ted and Alice's Oil Company or Ted and Alice's Bank opening on your street corner anytime soon.

In addition, we shouldn't always apply standards for business to government because the two are not the same in some important ways. For example, efficiency as a business concept doesn't translate well into the government context. In government you judge an agency not by its income statement but by its total cost-effectiveness on a society-wide basis. For example, people who complain that the US Postal Service "loses money" are not giving credit for the fact that it is a key part of our economic infrastructure and provides benefits to our economy and society that cannot be easily quantified and do not appear on an income statement. One could privatize that activity entirely, but if one company takes control over those logistics, wouldn't they wield a frightening amount of power over the market and the government? Again, efficiency in terms of saving money is not the only issue.

Private-sector people often look down on government people and call them incompetent, but ask yourself whether the problems that the government tries to solve are of the same type as those solved by most businesses. Is it the case that almost by definition the problems left unsolved by the private sector fall to the government? Would you rather build a better vacuum cleaner or solve homelessness? I'm just saying.

We should all recognize that whatever "don't tread on me" feelings we all have as Americans, the big picture is that business and the market system don't exist in a complete vacuum. The government must provide the rule of law; resolve disputes; enforce property rights and contract rights, antifraud, infrastructure, security, public health, and some part of education; and supervise a framework for private sector finance. Therefore, it isn't seemly for businesspeople to squawk about how they built the railroad all by themselves (that's actually a riff on an old Steve Landesberg joke that was far from politically correct). Give some credit to living in the USA, and you'll have a better reputation. If you benefit from a system that relies on the work of many people who are less fortunate than yourself, then be willing to give back, to be a little generous, if for no other reason than to demonstrate that you're not a complete jerk.

Any decision produces trade-offs, and government policy is no different. So don't be a glass-half-empty person. Be fair. Try to see the whole picture. Take the bad with the good. We get used to the system as it is, and we therefore tend to take it for granted. If we changed things the way some advocate, people might find that they don't like that either. The grass is always greener on the other side of the fence. We do not live in a perfect world and never will.

Finance and Accounting

Besides self-funding, there are four types of financing: equity, debt, insurance, and taxation. The financing method typically used by small business is debt, whether from a credit card, a credit line, or a business loan from a bank. The key is to generate revenues sufficient to repay the debt at the same time that you have enough profit to reinvest in the business and/or build a reserve. It isn't easy to do either, which is why a lot of businesses make no profits for the first few years. When borrowing money, remember that if you borrow too much at too high a rate, it can eat you alive. Do you really want to run that fast on a treadmill for that long so some bankers can build swimming pools in their backyards?

Because it can be hard to collect on moneys due to you at the same time that you owe money to other people, cash flow is a continuing problem for small business. By the way, if you owe money to a vendor and you can pay it right away, you should, because it is not their job to make short-term loans to you or anyone else. And if you are chronically slow at dealing with your payables, word could get around town about it. More importantly, because receivables are usually on the balance sheet and not on the income statement, if you rely on vendor financing "float" too much you may get a false sense of your financial position and this in turn can make errors in judgment more likely.

In addition to conventional borrowing from a bank, some finance firms will buy your receivables in a process we call factoring. Of course they will buy at a discount, so it is not optimal. By the way, securitization, the process that creates mortgage-backed and other asset-backed securities, is just an elaborate form of factoring. Debt instruments that represent the right to receive payments over time (receivables) are deposited in a trust, and certificates of participation in that trust are issued on the public capital markets. Often those certificates are structured in various ways to make some of them more marketable.

If a business issues equity (stock) or non-bank debt, it may trigger requirements under the securities laws. In fact, those laws have a very broad definition of a variety of things that are considered "securities."

Be aware of the time value of money. Because money can earn interest over time, money received today has more value than money received much farther into the future. The impact to a cash flow analysis depends on the level of the prevailing interest rates.

When I was a summer associate in a finance law firm in New York City, I was given an annual financial statement for CSX Corporation to look at. It puzzled me that the asset size number footed to the same number as the liability size. I asked a senior associate about that. He looked at me funny and asked: "What college did you go to?" The accounting equation is *assets = liabilities + owner's equity.* That implies then that *assets − liabilities = owner's equity.* The reason the two sides of the balance sheet are equal in value is that the left side represents what you own, and the right side represents what you owe or claims against what you own. This so-called "book value" is different from the values of the outstanding shares being traded at any given moment on the NYSE. A receivable is money owed to you and is an asset. A payable is money you owe to someone else and is a liability.

The income statement is easier and is simply *revenues − expenses = net income.* At the end of the reporting period, the net income goes into *owner's equity* on the balance sheet. An income statement is about the past—what happened—but it is similar to a budget projection. When budgeting, we are starting with our reserve (if any), adding the estimated revenues for the coming year (or whatever period is being used), and subtracting out the estimated expenses for the coming year, to arrive at a projected reserve balance at the end of the year. Also, we have to be mindful of cash flow in any given month or even week because we don't want to overdraft our bank account and draw on our credit lines if we can avoid that.

Sometimes we instruct novices that the balance sheet is like a photograph, a snapshot in time, whereas the income statement is more like a movie, watched over time.

Whatever subsidiary spreadsheets your internal accountant uses, they should all feed into and boil down to one single spreadsheet for the entire year where the columns are the twelve months and the rows are the items of revenues and expenses. Those of us who have investigated fraud know that fraudsters like to proliferate bank accounts and financial statements so that it is hard for anyone to see the big picture.

If you search the Internet you will find many glossaries of financial terms. There are also many lists of financial ratios. For example, ROR is Return on Revenues and means net income divided by total revenues. Another famous ratio is the Debt to Equity ratio, which tells you how much debt you have in relation to unencumbered assets. The Debt to Assets ratio is also commonly used.

I don't recommend putting any business assets into the financial markets, but if you do, remember one thing: you don't realize losses unless you actually sell the financial asset (in most cases). And obviously, before you buy a stock, you should check the current price against the price history on the Internet. And recognize that the value of fixed income debt instruments will change as the overall market interest rates fluctuate. And recognize the difference between being a long-term investor and a short-term trader. Although past performance does not predict future returns, long-term trends may be easier to predict than short-term trends because in the first case some of the continual volatility is "seen through."

Now, accountants are important, but business is partly about risk. It isn't uncommon for some businesses to experience years when they do not make a profit, such as when they are growing market share or developing new products. It is often shrewd to run "lean and mean," but you don't want to cut costs so much that you are too thinly staffed or begin to harm the quality of your product or service.

At the risk of getting into technicalities, accounting system details matter. I have seen a few companies that do not provide an invoice that states the current status of the account: showing what payment was last received by the company, what amount due has accrued in the past month, and what the net outstanding current balance due is. In other words, all the customer gets in the mail is a paper invoice that says what the current monthly amount due is, without any reconciliation as to the past. There are some laws that you may be violating with this kind of procedure if you're not careful. It is generally not the burden of the customer to prove that payment has been made if the check has been sent via US mail. It is the burden of the vendor to show that payment by the customer has *not* been made. If a vendor starts accusing a customer of being a deadbeat, and it is not true, the statements might be considered defamatory (or at least insulting). For everyone's benefit, your accounting system should credit payments made by the customer if you are billing on a recurring, periodic basis such as monthly.

Timing also matters. If I get an invoice, and I pay it that same day, and the next day I get an e-mail notice that I owe money, that's not good. And please, the timing of invoicing should be standardized. If I get an invoice and pay it, and then a week later I get another invoice when the services are supposed to be accruing on a monthly basis, that's not good. Again, execution matters. Or to put it another way, think of the billing as part of the total package of services that you are delivering (because it is). Evaluate the overall customer experience, including billing, because the last contact may be the basis of the impression they take away even if you have done very well up to that point.

CHAPTER 19
Hiring

Hiring the right person for the right job is the hardest part of running a business. As I said in my book *No More Stupidtry: Insights for the Modern World*, I think of television's *Mission Impossible*, where Peter Graves as Mr. Phelps sorts through photographs to pick his IMF team for each show. Observe that I said hiring for the "team," not simply for a given position description. In hiring people, I've sometimes been pleasantly surprised and sometimes horribly disappointed. I certainly don't think a paper résumé or a list of academic credentials can be taken as the whole story. In fact, the worst person I ever hired had a very high grade point average in college.

References can help, but skepticism is in order. Even when you have been around people a long time, you might not really see them for who they are. Some of us hide who we are. For example, remember Jem's surprise in the movie *To Kill a Mockingbird* when he finds out that his father, Atticus, is a good shot with a rifle. Some people are modest; others like the element of surprise. You never really know someone that well. That said, my feeling is that smart people can spot talent, and insecure people tend to deny or reject talent, and this is part of the reason that the fish rots from the head down.

I think our computer hiring systems and HR legal constraints are doing a disservice to us. If you see real talent, you should go out and recruit it. Waiting for talent to come to you is like a man in a restaurant sitting at a table and waiting for the beautiful woman across the room to come over and ask him for a date. It's just plain stupid, that's all. As to sending in an application, one should simply allow a PDF to be sent to an e-mail address and not require the navigation of a complex and semi-dysfunctional applicant-screening website. That is particularly true if you are trying to recruit upper level management talent. Those people have egos, and they want a little respect.

I like the idea of hiring ethical people, smart people, creative people (not the same thing as smart), funny people, and (most important) realistic people. But what really is most important? Candidates for the job should be able to talk about something they are passionate about. Without passion, the other faculties they may have can end up diffusing into the air. In addition, a complex system tends to produce specialists, so you have to scrutinize a person's background carefully. Donald Trump understands the real estate businesses, but does he understand product exporting? John McCain understands airpower, but does he understand ground assault? Does Mitt Romney understand marketing as well as finance? One of the great dangers is dealing with someone who is an expert in one area who thinks that he therefore knows a lot about other things. One needs to know what one doesn't know.

In addition to issues about experience, people have different personalities and preferences, and therefore their strengths and weaknesses are different. Someone who might do badly in one job could shine in another. Goodness of fit is the key. Or to put it the opposite way, ideally you want to find someone with a range of skills and interests so that if they are faced with new situations, they can learn and adapt quickly.

Promotion is a form of hiring. Obviously if you want to attract and retain meritorious employees, you need to run a meritocracy. Management guru Peter F. Drucker put it very well:

> If, however, Joe got promoted because he is a politician, everybody will know it. They will all say to themselves, Okay, that is the way to get ahead in this company. They will despise the management for forcing them to become politicians but will either quit or become politicians themselves in the end. As we have known for a long time, people in organizations tend to be influenced by the way they see others being rewarded. And when the rewards go to non-performance, to flattery, or to mere cleverness, the organization will soon decline into nonperformance, flattery, or cleverness. (*The Essential Drucker* [Harper, 2001], pages 134–135)

Now, the truth is that any manager foolish enough not to know this without being told is probably incompetent.

Historian Doris Kearns Goodwin emphasized Abraham Lincoln's wisdom in surrounding himself with a "team of rivals." Managers with fragile egos would rather surround themselves with people who will reassure them and not pop their bubble. While people with great talent sometimes hate the mediocre critics that pick at their work, it is nothing compared to the seething, deep-seated hatred that mediocrities sometimes hold in their hearts for people with great talent.

In chapter 1, I talked about execution and craftsmanship. The caveat is that perfectionism can slow people down, so you have to judge if the work you are doing requires perfection. If you're building a jet engine, it sure does. But not every task is equally sensitive. Also, if you don't have some tolerance for error, your team might be afraid to take risks or to innovate.

Finally, when hiring, recognize that not everyone has experience in making decisions or in watching money flow in and out. Some people are essentially drones who can do only very narrow tasks under supervision. Or maybe I should broaden that comment. Our system is complex, and as a result we tend to train people to be narrowly focused specialists. The problem is that when you are a hammer, everything looks like a nail. So you have to know your staff and what holes in your company's perceptual grid the limitations of their respective backgrounds create.

CHAPTER 20

IT Projects

IT projects are among the most difficult, the most expensive, and the hardest to reverse. You cannot delegate an IT project. You must lay hands on an IT project every single day to see what is going on and make sure there is forward progress. It helps if you can find some good protocols for doing IT projects before you start so that you don't just bungle along. Because of the giant gap in knowledge between IT people and other professionals, there is a constant challenge with communication and getting everyone on the same page. If I was a manager without IT knowledge and I had to do an IT project, I would hire someone with computer programming knowledge as an adviser because that person could spot issues that a normal professional cannot. If you have an internal IT department, they should have a basic questionnaire for taking in new projects. In addition, because planning and implementing changes to the IT system can take many years, one might want to periodically survey key managers to determine what their needs and goals are so that the IT professionals can keep their eyes open for a good solution.

Remember that unlike lawyers and accountants, IT professionals do not have any professional standards of conduct tied in to their licensing that they have to live up to. In fact, IT professionals are generally not licensed in the first place. As to software, there is often very little transparency from the vendor as to what is inside that black box.

The danger with IT is that the more customized programming you need to adapt off the shelf software for your organization, the more dependent on those programmers you will be. Once they get their hooks in you, be prepared to bleed money all over the place. It is not unlike a big public works project. Cost control is difficult because once the vendor knows that you can't walk away, the vendor has all the power. And the more integral the software is to your operations, the worse this problem is.

Some security experts say that cybersecurity is the number one national security risk. I agree. But we can do only so much because the hackers are often one step ahead of our solutions. You have to assume that data will be compromised, and therefore you do not want information like Social Security numbers (SSNs) to be attached to a hackable system. Consider retaining such sensitive information on a computer that is not attached to the Internet or on old-fashioned paper. You can use a proxy identification number to track your employee in the normal company database. If SSNs are compromised, it is very difficult to fix, and the consequential damage can be extensive. Be aware that data systems that anonymize data may not be entirely effective, at least not yet.

One unaddressed issue in IT work is that the legal staff and the IT staff are only now starting to realize that they need to talk to each other. What sometimes happens is that the IT system is developed in a way that is not consistent with the law. To fix it after the fact is usually impossible. You have to build the nexus between law and IT programming from the ground up. I suspect that it will be decades before the two areas of expertise find themselves in good cooperation. In addition, other stakeholders such as unions might have something to say about IT systems that enhance the monitoring of internal operations and processes.

Paper is a better technology than some give it credit for being, as is the US post office. Some people might want to do things the old-fashioned way, and I think it is optimal if a business can allow a workaround instead of saying, "That's not the way we do it." I understand that these workarounds can increase costs, but if you make the assumption that every customer matters, regardless of whether they use or can afford computers, then you will be maximizing revenues.

The law also requires that we recognize certain realities. If I send something via US mail, I'm not sure that a vendor can legally insist that I e-mail a PDF. If I want to pay cash, I'm not sure that a vendor can legally refuse the tender of that currency, although I suppose a vendor generally has the right to refuse service. I just don't think that "my way or the highway" is the way for a business to deal with its customers.

CHAPTER 21

CHAPTER
Futurist Thinking

Any businessperson must look forward into the future. Of course no one can really predict the future, but merely reacting to events as they transpire isn't the way to get ahead of your competitors. I'm not a soothsayer, and the past does not always predict the future, but I think there are some trends that will continue.

1. The world population will increase by more billions.
2. Environmental degradation will increase.
3. We will fight more over basic resources like water and key metals.
4. The culture of narcissism and the selfishness that it produces will continue, hampering leadership and weakening the glue that holds society and economies together.
5. We will become more dependent upon technology, despite the security risks to, and fragility of, the overall system that this approach often engenders.
6. Technology and science will continue to develop, including data analysis of human behavior and traits, increasing the potential for political and social control of the masses. Whether this enables totalitarianism depends on the strength of a

country's legal system and its cultural traditions and propensities. Our conceptions of privacy and intimacy will continue to change.

7. Increasing complexity of the system, particularly business regulation and information systems technology, will favor large business over small business and impede the formation of new businesses.

8. The days of the lifetime job with one company like IBM will become an even more distant memory. Some people will make money as economic vagabonds who continually reinvent themselves as they adapt quickly to changing circumstances. Robots and algorithms will force humans out of certain jobs of a more routine nature, and the question is whether there will be enough jobs to support the very large numbers of people on the planet. Think "independent contractor" more than "employee." Now to avoid creating too much fear around automation, when it comes to jobs that require continual learning and adaptation, humans will be cheaper than artificial intelligence for some time. Also, please note that if more people are economic vagabonds, that will affect politics because business owners and employees don't see the world the same way.

9. Most of us will continue the long march away from the Bible (and other ancient sacred texts) towards secularism and moral relativism.

10. Political and religious leaders in troubled societies will continue to try to retain power by projecting

and deflecting onto their favorite bogeymen (scapegoating). We would do well to remember that the rise of Adolf Hitler was due primarily not to a lack of political correctness but to a bad economy and the external and internal threat posed by communism.

11. Online retail will continue to damage local brick and mortar, adversely affecting local economies and changing patterns of movement and choice of residence. (Although note that in the old days we had a Sears mail order catalog and that two million small businesses sell through Amazon.) If the dream of a virtual office can be realized through technology, the need to move from small towns to large urban areas may reverse as more pastoral lifestyle choices become feasible. I suspect that one way to hold on to some brick and mortar is to go back (where possible) to the idea of a walking neighborhood where if you wanted to get something to eat or buy a few groceries you took a little walk and maybe saw a few of your neighbors along the way. Selling community as opposed to electronic alienation and atomization might be good business.

12. Assimilation of races and cultures will continue, but it won't always go well, and it won't happen quickly for some groups. Cultural assimilation is always a bit easier with people of roughly the same skin color because Daddy doesn't get as mad when his little girl brings home the wrong person. Sorry to have to say that, but sometimes gut reaction

overrides reason as a result of many thousands of years of evolution. Exposure and acclimatization helps—that is, you have to get used to diversity.

13. Demographics will continue to be destiny. Countries will high birthrates will produce a class of younger people that may feel disenfranchised. Countries with access to good public health and medical care will increase the cohort of older people. There may be a clash between the young and the old as the system attempts to accommodate their respective needs.

14. Pleasing voters in a democracy will sometimes produce bad outcomes if the government finds itself unable to ever say no. It is a good thing to be responsive to the public. It is disastrous to cater to their every whim and fancy. Once you start buying votes, you might find that you have to keep paying though the nose.

15. Inequality will continue to be driven partly by national and regional differences in (a) education and literacy, (b) the dispersion of information, (c) the adoption of superior technology, and (d) the use of the right kinds of political and financial institutions.

16. Globalization and modernization will continue, but not everyone will be happy about it. Some will want to return to a past seen through rose-colored glasses which never really was that great to begin with. Pockets of people will reject the new technologies and opt for the old ways of doing things and being, particularly when it comes time

to integrate computer technology into our bodies and brains.

17. There will be an ongoing tension between national regulatory systems and an increasingly networked global market. The desire of some for uniformity in governance will run full speed into the problem of governing structures that are too big to function properly and can impede innovation.

18. The invention of the "Virtual Spouse" will obviate the need to deal with an irritating husband or wife and will give people the chance to marry any Hollywood star or runway model from the past and change things up as they like. There may even be "sexbots" which will raise interesting issues, such as how they can be delivered to a buyer without raising questions from the neighbors and whether someone who prefers a sexbot that is more like R2D2 is more deviant than someone who prefers a sexbot that looks more like a real person. And as lawyer, frankly, I can't say that I like the products liability issues.

19. Lawyers will pioneer an important new basis for divorce lawsuits, which will be labeled "the intentional infliction of emotional distress and alienation of affection due to my spouse having sexual relations with me while talking on their smart phone or watching a video on their Google glasses."

20. Children will be partly replaced by robots because the education system has become far too expensive

for anyone to have real children. A couple might have one real child and a few robot children to keep the real one company. (These last three are just jokes; don't get any ideas!)

I admit that these forecasts sound a bit pessimistic, but one has to keep an eye out for landmines. As the Chinese saying goes—"where there is great danger, there is great opportunity." Hopefully, things go better than my list suggests. It is difficult to predict what the human capacity for problem solving and innovation will produce down the road. My main purpose in calling out these issues is to make sure we get animated and act as though our survival depends on all of us keeping on our toes and pulling our weight, because (of course) it does.

CHAPTER 22
Suggestions for Further Business Reading

For simple general advice on an approach to life, try *Secret Millionaires Club: Warren Buffet's 26 Secrets to Success in the Business of Life* by Andy and Amy Heward or *Success: The Glenn Bland Method* by Glenn D. Bland or *Screw It, Let's Do It: Lessons in Life* by Richard Branson.

For advice on thinking outside the box, try *A Whack on the Side of the Head: How You Can Be More Creative* by Roger von Oech.

For leadership, try *The Leader's Bookshelf* by Adm. James Stavridis and R. Manning Ancell, *What Successful People Know about Leadership* by John C. Maxwell, and *Churchill* by Paul Johnson. The third book in that list is a biography.

For a basic introduction to economics, try *Economics: A Very Short Introduction* by Partha Dasgupta and *How the Economy Works: Confidence, Crashes and Self-Fulfilling Prophecies* by Roger E. A. Farmer. For a critique and defense of economics, try *Economics Rules: The Rights and Wrongs of the Dismal Science* by Dani Rodrik. For a comprehensive economics textbook, try *Macroeconomics* by N. Gregory Mankiw. For a brief economic history of the United States, try *The Economic Transformation of America: 1600 to the Present* by Robert Heilbroner and Aaron Singer. If you want a cheat sheet/executive summary of economics, try my four-and-a-half-page chapter on economics in my book *Basic Stuff That Everyone Should Know.*

For business relationships, try *How to Win Friends and Influence People* by Dale Carnegie.

For marketing/communications, try *Made to Stick: Why Some Ideas Survive and Others Die* by Chip Health and Dan Heath.

For a comprehensive finance textbook, try *Finance Markets and Institutions: A Modern Perspective* by Anthony Saunders and Marcia Millon Cornett. Also good are the audio/DVD courses by Connel Fullencamp available from The Great Courses.

For an entertaining novel about business ups and downs and their effect on a person's identity, try *Tono-Bungay* by H G Wells. If you don't have time to read and prefer to watch a movie, try *Wall Street* directed by Oliver Stone and *Other People's Money* directed by Norman Jewison. They have similar themes, but the first is drama and the second is comedy.

For a basic understanding of the government, try *United States Government: Democracy in Action* by Richard C. Remy. Because it is a textbook, it is pricey, but it will provide a solid foundation to build on.

For a concise treatment of the intellectual and cultural soup that forms part of the foundation of our society, try my book *No More Stupidtry: Insights for the Modern World*. Why might you want to read this? Because context matters. Because developing one's perceptual grid matters.

CHAPTER 23

Philosophical Musings

Business is who we are, from the first caveman that killed a tapir and offered the meat to his girlfriend and child in the cave, to the trading of commodities futures on a computer exchange today. Those who deny that and who hate the productive magic that is the market system are people who fundamentally don't like people. Watch out for misanthropes and America-haters who claim to be good-hearted idealists. As Calvin Coolidge put it: "The chief business of the American people is business." The day that changes is the day we condemn ourselves to eating cockroaches for dinner.

One of the reasons why Western civilization separated church and state is to facilitate the market. No businessperson has time to figure out the past conduct of their customers, let alone their internal thinking or values. If someone has green money to exchange for what you are selling, it may not do to be too picky (although clearly products are not the same as services in this regard).

As long as a business exchange is voluntary, which assumes no government mandate and sufficient competition or alternatives when necessities are involved, then these exchanges should not be thought of as immoral. On the other hand, if people sometimes feel as if the system turns them into mice running endlessly on a treadmill as they pay through the nose for education, housing, food, and medical care, among other things, they might have a point. But what do we want? Do we all want to just sit around and accomplish nothing? Work is dignity and identity and purpose. As to whether it is inherently meaningful, no business can survive long without helping someone, but meaning is beside the point because it implies that work is supposed to make you happy. Be happy in your ability to do the job well, but don't expect a deeper philosophical meaning. We work to live, like our ancestors before us.

Some people hate the "social Darwinism" of capitalism, so let me clarify something. Natural selection in the Darwinian sense doesn't exist very much anymore with respect to human beings. Most people live and reproduce, regardless of merit. In the days of the saber-toothed cat, a guy like me with horrible eyesight would have been eaten long before impregnating a mate.

Today, the idea of survival of the fittest doesn't necessarily mean survival of the strongest. Being well fit to a situation sometimes means being a giant nerd with horn-rimmed glasses and skimpy muscles. The Nazis thought they were the strongest and the best, but where are they now? I think the concept of social Darwinism is meaningless, so perhaps we should just relegate it to the dustbin of history.

Elites always find ways of justifying their elite status, but that doesn't mean that the theories they use are valid. Being the richest doesn't necessarily mean that you are the smartest or the most knowledgeable or even that you're a decent economist. That said, I think being rich generally beats being poor, even if it doesn't solve everything and can even create certain problems for you. Anyway, Andrew Carnegie gave his money away, and so can you. As to those who secretly dream of being part of an all-powerful plutocracy that rules over a multitude who are functionally enslaved, let me suggest that such a system is not politically stable and probably won't generate enough aggregate demand to make for a truly prosperous society.

What is the takeaway for those aspiring to be rich? Someone once said that other people are not going to get in your way as much as you're going to get in your own way. Sir Richard Branson's formulation couldn't be simpler: "Just do it. Think yes, not no" (*Screw It, Let's Do It: Lessons in Life* [Virgin Books 2006], page 103). If you don't want to believe me, then believe Branson (he's actually rich). Branson is the eternal optimist, and it could be a significant factor in his business success.

Also, however people may criticize President Donald Trump, observe that he pats himself on the back for his achievements and treats himself to some rewards. There is a lesson in that. I call it self-induced positive reinforcement. He is his own Skinner box, as it were. The takeaway is that attitude matters or, as my business card says, actions follow ideas. If you see yourself as a victim or a loser, then that's what you'll be. You have to believe in yourself and know in your heart that the United States of America is the greatest country in the history of the world. Don't get in your own way. Some folks may be critical of capitalism, but as has often been observed before—-capitalism is the best system we have invented so far in terms of its practical effects, in spite of its imperfections and excesses.

Not to undercut the pro-business messages in this book, I like to recall a conversation I had with a friend when I was a teenager. We were talking about being rich. I said that I wanted to be rich one day. My friend said that he didn't want to be rich because he wanted to have friends. He didn't like the idea of being isolated. Interesting perspective for a student, don't you think? We don't normally think of affluence as an intellectual and social ghetto, but in its own way, it can be. Handling money can be tricky. As Sir Francis Bacon put it: "Money makes a good servant, but a bad master."

How to resolve this dilemma? By regarding wealth as the incidental by-product of activity done for another purpose. Two of our past presidents have spoken in similar terms on this topic. Thomas Jefferson said: "It is neither wealth nor splendor, but tranquility and occupation, which gives happiness." Franklin Delano Roosevelt said: "Happiness lies not in the mere possession of money; it lies in the joy of achievement, in the thrill of creative effort."

We work to live, but we also live to work. As to the purpose of that work and whether it is done to serve the greater glory of God or increase Satan's reach over a sinful world, I will leave those matters to you, dear reader. I ask only one thing: remember that the reason the West separated church and state and removed theocracy was because it was bad for business. I lied. I ask for one more thing: remember that using the government and the law to erect protectionist barriers to insulate your business from market forces will make our country weaker on the global stage over the long term.

I have tremendous respect for the best companies in the United States. They're not just good at what they do; they're great. I never cease to be amazed at what they make possible for the rest of us. Like most American consumers, I'm horribly spoiled by that; my expectations are through the roof. So if you decide to go into business, just be aware that you have to stay on your toes and be at the top or your game at all times. Yankee know-how. Watch out for those folks when they get their dander up! I am like a child in wonderland when I walk through a Lowe's, Home Depot or Wal-Mart. The cornucopia of choices is simply amazing to me, particularly when compared with the empty shelves of the old Soviet Union. Sometimes I think our perspective is skewed just a little bit. When I fly on a commercial airline, it blows me away to think about how quickly I am able to cover land that at one time people navigated by covered wagon. We get irritated because a flight is delayed an hour, but when compared with what used to be, and in light of the massive logistics involved in moving as many people as we do every day—our air travel system is nothing short of a miracle.

Here's a key question: what would you rather be? Would you rather be someone who dresses like a bum but has a lot of money or someone who dresses like a fashionista and is constantly in debt? Would you rather own a company that was really big, but had big debt and negative net income or would you rather own a company that was small and had very little debt and positive net income? Don't judge a book by its cover. Sometimes substance over style can be good business. As the old saying goes: "get rich by acting poor." As my church pastor David Rivers has written: "Is the pursuit of prestige a mirage that is ever shifting and changing, which gives us a false sense of reality, instead of the richness of His Kingdom? May you discover the freedom of living in your own skin and being okay with your true self!" The way I pose the question is this: *is that your job or your Gucci bag?* Should it be very surprising that there may be a rough correlation between worldly success and not being a phony, when business is about relationships?

Afterword

I want to leave you with a single piece of advice that is a corollary to the KISS rule (keep it simple, stupid): beware of people with complex minds who like to build complex contraptions, whether mechanical or verbal. A smart person thinks in a straight line and cuts right through the fog like a laser beam. Complexity of thought often indicates stupidity or perhaps even a perverse love of the chaos that complexity often creates. As expressed so well by Albert Einstein: "Everything should be made as simple as possible, but no simpler."

Remember this: if you are thinking about solving your own problems, you're more like a customer or an employee; if you're thinking about solving the problems of others, you're on your way to becoming a true businessperson.

And so, to recap: *business involves offering something that people want to buy for a price they are willing to pay and then inducing buying behavior.*

Problem? Easier said than done.

Bibliography

Bardach, Eugene, and Eric M. Patashnik, *A Practical Guide for Policy Analysis,* vol. 5, Sage, 2016.

Becker, Alfred, *The 10 Pillars of Wealth: Mind-Sets of the World's Richest People*, Brown Books, 2016.

Branson, Richard, *Screw It, Let's Do It: Lessons in Life*, Virgin Books, 2006.

Collins, Jim, *Good to Great: Why Some Companies Make the Leap and Others Don't*, Harper Business, 2001.

Drucker, Peter F., *The Essential Drucker*, Harper, 2001.

Fried, Jason, and David Heinemeier Hansson, *Rework*, Crown Business, 2010.

Marcus Aurelius, *Meditations*, Dover Thrift Editions, Dover Publications 1992.

Maxwell, John C., *What Successful People Know About Leadership*, Center Street, 2016.

Nichols, Tom, "How Americans Lost Faith in Expertise," *Foreign Affairs* (March/April 2017).

Oreck, David, *From Dust to Diamonds: How Small Entrepreneurs Can Grow and Prosper in Any Economy*, TAG, 2013.

Smith, Gary V., *The NIV Application Commentary: Hosea, Amos, Micah,* Zondervan, 2001.

Stroh, David P., *Systems Thinking for Social Change*, Chelsea Green, 2015.

Zimmermann, Jens, *Hermeneutics: A Very Short Introduction*, Oxford, 2015.

Two audio/DVD courses from The Learning Company/ The Great Courses:

Patrick Grim, *The Philosopher's Toolkit: How to Be the Most Rational Person in Any Room*, 2013.

Steven Novella, *Your Deceptive Mind: A Scientific Guide to Critical Thinking Skills*, 2012.

Fifteen Basic Work Principles

1. Emphasize craftsmanship, not intelligence. Hard work and refined skills can beat raw intelligence. Think improvement, not stagnation.

2. Guard your credibility. Making a mistake doesn't hurt credibility as much as lying about making a mistake. The big problem is often not the crime, it's the cover-up.

3. Show that you are someone who can follow instructions. Before doing, make sure you understand the assignment.

4. Think critically about the difference between what you know and don't know. If you don't know, find out more. When doing so, consider the reliability of the source.

5. Remember that e-mail is hackable and discoverable in litigation. Write as if it would appear on the front page of the newspaper. Otherwise, pick up the phone.

6. Don't make accusations or assume bad faith. Be aware of impliedly doing so through your actions.

7. Don't leave customers hanging because it is insulting to their human dignity.

8. Think before acting or speaking.

9. Follow up and follow through.

10. Understand that just because someone outside your firm asks you a question, that doesn't mean you have to answer or even that you are the right person to answer.

11. Foster the impression in your customers that you understand and care about their needs.

12. In meetings, listen carefully, and keep up with where the conversation is now. Playing with devices or taking notes can impede listening as much as daydreaming.

13. Know what is going on around you; keep up with current events; scan the horizon.

14. The best laid plans go astray, but preparation is necessary for decent improvisation.

15. To be early is to be on time, to be on time is to be late, and to be late is inexcusable. Arrive early, and benefit from informal conversations.

Thirty Advanced Organizational Behavior Concepts

1. Life is a journey, and people develop over that time. Although you may be more or less who you are now, there is always room for development, but it can take a long time and requires effort and dedication. What does that mean? It means that if you make a mistake, it doesn't have to define the rest of your life if you are willing to do what is

needed to learn from the experience and improve. Mistakes can be called "learning experiences."

2. Criticism from a manager can hurt, but it is often done to try to help you improve. Ask yourself if you would rather get zero feedback and then one day simply get fired. Consider the benefits of a thick skin. We all make mistakes, but anyone can be legitimately criticized for not trying to do better (assuming they have the capability).

3. Before you go into a meeting, don't you want to know what the purpose of the meeting is and who is going to be there? That way you can do a little preparation.

4. Even when we get a bad outcome, we can defend by having a reasonable process and procedure.

5. Speed of execution is always an issue for a variety of reasons: (a) people work at different speeds; (b) some tasks are more complex than others and require more time to develop, while others are more routine; (c) some tasks/goals have a higher priority; (d) to avoid building a "queue" or a "pile," it sometimes is better to do things that can be done fast first and let more complex things run their course over time, but on the other hand, sometimes you should do the important things first so that they get done and let things of less consequence wait. In other words, there is no hard and fast rule about speed, and one has to use judgment on the order of execution based on the situation.

6. Be aware of the volume of your voice when talking on the phone or to co-workers in the office because it can be disturbing. If you have a personal call, it may be better to take it outside the office. No conversation is private (what you say can be repeated to others).

7. Recognize that sometimes people's behavior is due not just to their personalities, but to the situation they find themselves in. the point is not to excuse bad behavior but to understand it better by putting it in context.

8. Recognize the limitations of walking a mile in another's moccasins. If you have always been an employee, it can be hard to fully understand what it is like to be a business owner or even a staff manager. This is also why some politicians and government workers at times do things to businesses that are very dysfunctional—they have never run a business themselves. They know not what they do.

9. Recognize that those who profit from grievance will tend to want to prolong the underlying problem.

10. When dealing with data, be aware of the date and statistical significance of the data and the difference between direct and indirect correlation. Misattribution of causation can result in misidentification of the cause of a problem and a waste of time and money. Also, be wary of extrapolating beyond the data and predicting the future based on past data.

11. Be aware of cognitive biases: observation bias, confirmation bias, and hindsight bias (among many others). Recognize that interpretation is always occurring, and some subjectivity is always involved.

12. Know that the vanity and denial resulting from people's attempts to protect their fragile and oversized egos can significantly distort their perceptions of reality.

13. Watch out for projection—both projecting your own "stuff" onto others and others projecting their "stuff" onto you.

14. Don't believe everything you hear. Run a fact check or verification procedure if you're not sure about the reliability of the source of the information. Reality testing. Know when you should read the original text and not rely on secondary sources.

15. Know what you don't know. Recognize that you might not even know what you don't know. Donald Rumsfeld called this "the unknown unknowns." Listen, unless you know it all.

16. Understand the difference between correlation and causation. Just because it rains when I step outside, that doesn't mean that one caused the other.

17. Understand that not everything is the same thing. Recognize that analogies tend to break down the closer you scrutinize the facts. Recognize that although you can answer two different questions

the same way, you don't have to because they're not the same question.

18. Managing diversity includes making people feel comfortable that there is a level enough playing field that they don't have to cheat.

19. Standing up for oneself doesn't require fighting every single fight. Know the difference between important and unimportant, big and small, and pick your battles. Sometimes it makes sense to stay above the fray.

20. Watch out for theory versus practice. Facts matter, context matters. Although reality changes and can be changed with action, we must take reality for what it is at any given moment. We can dream about the future but not about the present or the past.

21. Every member of the team is important. Being farther down in a hierarchy doesn't reduce the need for excellent execution. As Lincoln put it: "Whatever you are, be a good one."

22. In assessing risk, remember that the two variables are severity and frequency. You may be facing a very severe consequence, but if the probability of occurrence is very low, it may be worth encountering/assuming that risk. You cannot completely eliminate risk, and you cannot completely predict the future.

23. If questions arise, you can always ask your boss. Sometimes we answer our own questions without even realizing that we are doing that. Talking to others and bouncing things off of them (vetting)

is a way of checking that our thinking is on target. You can call it a form of reality testing. And make sure you're asking the right kind of person to do the vetting.

24. When leaving voice mail, start with your name, organization, and phone number before any lengthy message. That way if they have to repeat the message, they don't have to wait through the entire recording. What is the advanced concept in this trivial matter? Be considerate of others. Think about something other than yourself; it may pay unexpected dividends. Also, when leaving a phone message, ask yourself whether right after that you should leave your desk or move on to another call. Some people use an answering machine to screen calls, and some may be occupied only briefly, and it can be annoying to call back and leave a message and then wait a long time for a response. Why? Because "Hey, you called me."

25. Before communicating (or acting, for that matter) think through four basic layers: (a) ethics/morality; (b) professionalism; (c) politics/ diplomacy/politeness; (d) plain old "common" sense—is it smart?

26. Any serious communication should be responded to in a timely way—if it calls for a response and if you are the right person in the organization to respond.

27. Whether to use a phone, an e-mail, an office visit, or a letter to execute a communication is an important decision.

28. E-mail is tricky because people get a lot of e-mails, and they usually read them at high speed and not very carefully. Therefore, if you want to control the reply to any problem, consider a two-step procedure: send an e-mail to the intended recipients first, and then forward that e-mail to those others whom you want to copy. Also, be aware that you can send "invisible" e-mail by e-mailing yourself and blind copying the people you want to tell: the recipients won't see the names of the others on the e-mail list. And there are other e-mail procedural tricks that one can use. The tricky thing is that different e-mail systems have different displays, and you're never completely sure how the reader is seeing the addresses. Certain internal e-mail protocols can also be surprising. And don't forget that merely deleting an e-mail is usually ineffective in the sense that it probably can be retrieved from somewhere with enough effort. And watch out for the "chain of custody" issue. There is a big difference between forwarding a document attached to someone else's e-mail and detaching the document to send it with your own e-mail. It raises issues of authentication and authorization and what is in that draft of the document. And of course, realize that there is no security or privacy that can be assured with respect to any

e-mail, even a "deleted" e-mail (which is often recoverable). E-mails should be polite. When I see e-mails that are rude, it sometimes suggests to me that the sender is emotional and out of control. People that routinely take their frustrations out on others probably don't belong in a standard work environment. Also, if your email is urgent remember that people are busy and don't always get to their emails right away, so you may want to follow up by leaving a brief voice mail to the effect that you just sent an important email.

29. At one time I believed that an interoffice memorandum could make recommendations by arguing both sides of a question. Then I read some writings by St. Thomas Aquinas and realized that this methodology might be too confusing. Still, even if you make a one-sided argument, you should also flag any issues or concerns and disclose evidence that is contrary to your position. It is a way of helping the decision-maker get it right, but it is also a way of protecting yourself from criticism that may blow back on you later if things go wrong.

30. For some meetings, you may want to have a witness so that people don't put words in your mouth, misremember, or accuse you of a sexual assault that did not occur. Back in the days of Mayberry RFD, this might have been unnecessary, but today? The other side of it is that if there is more than one person in a meeting, don't expect to assert confidentiality with regard to anything you

say. Public statements are (sometimes/often) fair game for repetition. As the Ben Franklin saying goes: "Three may keep a secret, if two of them are dead."

31. Sometimes the use of a smartphone (or similar device) isn't really "smart." To me, trying to talk on the phone while doing something else, like reading or driving or buying lunch or playing the piano or doing open heart surgery, is equivalent to having your head jammed all the way up your arse. Some busybodies think that talking on a smart phone while they are supposed to be doing something else makes them look important. You know: "I'm on the horn with Cape Canaveral, I'm on the horn!" Here's a news flash: "busy" doesn't mean "important," and it doesn't mean "thinking." And ask yourself whether you really want to pick up the phone and talk to everyone who might call you. In the old days, executives had secretaries who screened calls. One benefit is that it gives you a chance to consider whether you need to prepare for the call before talking to someone. If a caller broadsides you with questions and you haven't had a chance to think through a response, you might make a mistake by deciding something off the top of your head. Now, you can always say, "Let me think about it and get back to you," but in my experience we humans are not always perfect when deciding off the top of our heads which items need to receive that treatment and which don't.

Nine Goal-Setting Precepts

1. Make sure you distinguish the task of identifying goals from the task of identifying internal firm problems. There is more to long-term strategic goal-setting (which is a positive proposition) than solving internal firm problems (which is more of a negative proposition). We always have a goal to solve problems, but there must also be other goals.

2. Distinguish strategic goals from measurement. Benchmarking is not a goal—it's a measurement of progress toward a goal. The definitions of words matter.

3. Goals, ideas, aspirations, dreams, and theories are all important, but until you move into implementation—specifically the creation of practical tools that people could actually use in the ordinary course of business—ideation is meaningless.

4. In generating goals, consider process: issue spotting, pro and con analysis, devil's advocates, nonjudgmental brainstorming sessions, and use of facilitators.

5. Setting a goal is a different task from fostering motivation in people to work toward that goal. Change often meets resistance, and getting buy-in takes work and a good understanding of communication issues. Remember FDR: we have nothing to fear but fear itself. It takes confidence, even faith, to take risks. Change can't happen without the right leadership.

6. There isn't a bright line between setting goals and sketching out an implementation plan. Sometimes getting the big picture right requires knowledge of certain details. Thus, a key step is that at some point you need to get the right people around the table. That means that all needed basic areas of expertise are present.

7. Carefully examine your assumptions about what is a desirable goal. For example, people often have "efficiency" as a goal, but would you really want the criminal justice system to be more efficient? Don't slowness, due process, and deliberation count for something in that situation? It can be all too easy to assume away these "values" issues and end up harming yourself in the long run.

8. The persons principally responsible for seeing a goal through implementation are the board of directors and the CEO. So the board must take a minute to assess what is and is not in the head of the CEO, and if some material deficiency relates to the core mission of the organization, then remedial action is needed. Most people like to pretend they know things when they don't, and that can be perilous for anyone who wants to succeed.

9. Consider how you are going to determine or measure whether the goal has been met and whether deadlines along the way can be imposed.

Twelve Principles for Fostering Motivation

1. People have their own reasons for doing things, so don't assume they're doing things for you or because of your great leadership. That said, most people would like to believe that their work serves a larger purpose, whether it is duty to family or to the mission of the organization. People also tend to like challenges because they create the opportunity to show off skills and achievement.

2. You have to avoid anyone treating some people like peons. Every member of the team must understand that their contribution, however small, is crucial to success—because it is, particularly when the deadlines are tight.

3. If you have never done the other person's job, then don't assume it is that easy. Monday morning quarterbacking is done by couch potatoes.

4. The best motivation is to take pleasure in the fine execution of a task.

5. Every decision involves trade-offs, so it may not make sense to be a "Debbie downer," glass-half-empty type of person.

6. Bold action requires faith in the future and confidence in one's environment. It may also require tolerance for error and failure.

7. The ego and vanity of the leader may be demotivating for the staff. The idea behind "servant leadership" or "leader as vendor" is simply that you can't lead by your position title—leadership must come from within you.

8. Don't expect automatic loyalty or respect—these things have to be earned, just like everything else.

9. Criticizing someone is often best done in private. For every such action, there is an equal and opposite reaction—we call it "pushback" or "blowback." Also, if you turn out to be wrong and you have gone public, then you might have to do a public retraction and mea culpa. In addition, people tend to have families and at least some friends and allies, so if you attack someone, you might incur the hostility of more than just that person. Constantly beating up on an employee tends to be highly demotivating and psychological studies from the operant conditioning field show that punishment is less effective than reward in changing behavior.

10. Zero tolerance usually doesn't make sense when dealing with flawed humans, unless the offense is extremely serious. Zero tolerance is demotivating and hypocritical.

11. Inconsistency in a manager or leader can be demotivating.

12. There are different kinds of intelligence and different styles of learning, so people need a little room to be themselves.

Four Key Points in Market Analysis

1. Know the difference between prices and costs.
2. Know the difference between a buyer and a seller.
3. Know the difference between supply and demand and how the interaction of the two affects price.
4. Know that the economy is composed of many different markets (or submarkets).

Four Key Points in Marketing Strategy

1. The product or service puts parameters around your marketing strategy.
2. Recognize that your brand (differentiating the name and image) is not the same as the message.
3. Your message must be simple and grab attention.
4. Know your target market and tailor your message to it.

Eleven Questions to Spark Thinking

1. Can the truth or falsity of a statement be determined by reference to the identity, status, or motives of the speaker? Answer: No, they are irrelevant to a statement's truth or falsity; we only rely on them in the absence of facts.
2. Do we learn about the past (history, culture) to avoid repeating it? Answer: No, history doesn't repeat itself on all facts. We learn about the past to refine our perceptual grids and to improve

our ability to derive meaning from and interpret what we see, experience, and read in a more discerning way.

3. Is there a universally agreed upon meaning about what science is? Answer: No; in fact there is a whole academic area devoted to that issue.

4. Was Ralph Waldo Emerson right when he said that "a foolish consistency is the hobgoblin of little minds"? Answer: Debate it!

5. Do strong convictions make a person right? Answer: No.

6. Is there a clear line dividing fact from opinion? Answer: Sometimes, but not always.

7. Is information sharing good or bad? Answer: It depends, but people need certain information to do their jobs.

8. How can process protect you? Answer: by providing a fallback defense when the outcome is bad; and before that hopefully improving the likelihood that the outcome is good.

9. Is there any truth to the whispers from the cornfield in the movie *Field of Dreams* that "If you build it, they will come"? Answer: sometimes, but not typically.

10. Is it safer to make a normative statement or a descriptive statement? Answer: descriptive, because fact is safer than opinion.

11. Is there any danger in using analogies? Answer: yes, because close examination often shows that the analogy breaks down; i.e., analogies tend to be superficial.

Twenty Steps toward a Successful IT Project

1. Define the problem to be solved.

2. Define the project objective/purpose (do due diligence, consult users, determine types of documents or tasks implicated, determine current organization of documents or data, determine existing work flows and movements of documents or data, separate human interaction from IT support).

3. Before designing the system, ask yourself what the user needs, and understand that the user may not know everything, including some of the things lawyers and forensic accountants would need if they have to look at things after the fact.

4. Before designing the system, ask yourself what kind of metadata and meta-analysis both management and any ex post investigators/examiners will need.

5. Recognize that IT systems can enable tasks and provide support, but also that they can become a constraint. In particular, it can be difficult to change them once they are set up, so if you need operations to stay dynamic and flexible, automation may end up hurting you in the end.

6. Realize that knowing whether software will work for you is impossible without vigorous on-site testing; for software you may need to build a model.

7. Understand what kinds of paper should be maintained as a backup; ask if there is a simpler solution than one based on IT.

8. Define the project scope; consider the need for a pilot/proof of concept before full implementation.

9. Do a preliminary sketch of a solution to the problem, ask what change in work flows or document flows is desired, what changes in staff behavior are desired, and what monitoring by management is desired.

10. Do a preliminary sketch of document and content governance policies to meet document retention and audit requirements.

11. Step back and ask: does the solution solve the problem and meet the objective/purpose?

12. Brainstorm: reality test, issue spot, consider alternative paths, general vetting, and venting.

13. Consider the future of obsolete systems and platforms, transitioning databases, and life cycles.

14. Set project management control structures and parameters.

15. Determine what procurement is needed/appropriate.

16. Determine any special criteria needed for project vendor(s).

17. Draft summary and get preliminary approvals.

18. Create implementation/action plan, including project life cycle, roles and responsibilities, communication plan, and a rough time line to estimate completion of various aspects and phases of the project, and identify any critical path issues.

19. Seek approval of plan, begin procurement, and begin project.
20. Remember that computer people and non–computer people speak different languages, and bridging the gap needs constant attention.

Eleven Principles for Orienting toward Government

1. Business often takes a position of neutrality on political issues, and rightly so. The market system is usually indifferent to the identity or beliefs of sellers.

2. There is business opportunity in government contracts and grants, but there are usually strings attached.

3. When talking to government people, be ready to put on your kneepads. Some might have a few insecurities, and you don't want to pull the scab off the wound. If they have authority and jurisdiction to act, then don't question that part of it.

4. Don't create work unnecessarily for government bureaucrats. Be brief. Know when a question has been asked and answered.

5. If you are going to complain about a government decision or policy, be able to articulate an alternative. There is no perfect world; every decision involves trade-offs one way or the other,

and you are exchanging one set of problems for another.

6. If you find yourself complaining that government isn't run like a business, check your facts: the government isn't a business.

7. In thinking about the partisan divide, go back and listen to "Gee, Officer Krupke" from *West Side Story.*

8. To get a ruling on a law, one usually needs a specific set of facts to apply the law to (i.e., a "case"). Law doesn't operate on the basis of generalities and abstractions. We lawyers need a "case."

9. Recognize that there is no such thing as a world with no government, any more than there can be a world with no market. The question is the balance and the calibration.

10. You can't assume that government managers or public board members can determine an approach to a new project or problem, or even that they know how to fill the gaps in their knowledge before they run off and do something. So if you plan on doing a public-private partnership, it is worth making sure that the managers on the public side know what they don't know and talk to some folks with the relevant expertise *before* they develop an approach.

11. Don't assume that criticizing or undermining a politician is the way to get what you want. Sometimes they need support, including help with developing the right arguments to use to

justify a policy, and with research to figure out the consequences of a policy. Many politicians have a deep-seated need to be liked, and this makes them susceptible to bad influences, so if you can stiffen their spine by being a friend, sometimes it works better than turning them into enemies. No one likes to look bad, particularly in front of a large audience like the general public. They are trying to find a path in the midst of various interests that are pushing and pulling them in different directions. It's not that easy to manage. And I can tell you that fairly often politicians and other high government officials get blamed for things that are more or less outside their control. They may just need a friendly reminder that when you try to please everybody, you end up pleasing nobody. I'm not trying to justify the incompetence and duplicity that we see a lot of the time from politicians. I'm just saying.

Five Key Writing Tips

1. Writing can often be improved by following Strunk & White's rule number 17: "Omit needless words," which simply means to write concisely, with economy and efficiency. Someone once said that if you're not doing revisions, you're not a writer, and that is partly true. No one gets it right on the first pass. Composing on a computer is fine, but when revising, first doing a hand markup of a

printout is a best practice. Proofreader's marks can be found in the dictionary and on the Internet.

2. One should consider the audience and the author's purpose and then take the reader on a tour of the writer's thinking. The style depends on the situation, but sometimes it is a good idea to separate facts from opinions to avoid confusing the audience. There are many audiences, not just your intended/target audience, so you should consider the different ways your writing might be interpreted because words are always subject to interpretation. For example, one day your writing may end up in front of a jury.

3. Rhetorical tricks can be used to protect the writer's credibility. If there is uncertainty, sometimes stating issues/questions is better than impetuously drawing conclusions. When dealing with something that is not an absolutely provable fact, you can usually still fashion words in such a way as to make the statement sound like a fact or be more defensible based on the evidence. In other words, if one is challenged, one might want to be able to back up one's statements with evidence. In other words, calibrate, calibrate, calibrate.

4. It will be difficult to write interesting and accurate material unless you read a lot and keep abreast of current events. Double-check your facts after you write so you aren't going only on your memory.

5. Now a procedural point. If you're doing multiple drafts and working with a group of readers, put a draft number and draft date on the document. Don't

rely on the date of the e-mail to solve the problem. And sometimes if you use the computer to mark the document to show changes, it will save the reader time. People's time is precious, so you want to keep the number of drafts down to a minimum. Also, proliferation of drafts can create confusion.

Eight Cardinal Rules

1. **If you don't know money in and money out pretty much every day, then you're more likely to be a bureaucrat than a businessperson.** Your inside accountant should be able to show you a single spreadsheet that has the entire year to date (YTD) income and expense reporting. There will be subsidiary spreadsheets that feed into that, but the cumulative or aggregate is what you need to see the big picture.

2. **Remember that a person's greatest strengths are often their greatest weaknesses**. Goodness of fit for the situation depends partly on the person but also partly on the situation. The traits that make someone perfect for one situation may make them ineffective in another situation. But we're all mixed bags, so one probably has to take the good with the bad and show loyalty and reciprocity when they are due. That said, the reason this rule about strengths and weaknesses can be important is that these traits may also be the person's predominant trait.

3. **Don't attack people who aren't doing anything wrong**. If you do, you will look like a nutcase. People who are evil tend to over-perceive evil in others. People who nitpick others, when they themselves are full of faults and make their fair share of errors, are dreaming themselves to be gods. People who are addicted to hurting others for pleasure are not going to be well liked by anyone. In other words, if you're a sick puppy, do everyone a favor and just stay home.

4. **Personnel may be policy, but they are never perfect, so you need procedures**. Picking the right person for the job is the key, but given the range and complexity of some jobs and the narrowness of the way people are trained, top management always needs to think about procedures that can both create a good approach without putting minds into a straightjacket and create a defensible position in litigation.

5. **Being decisive includes deciding when to be decisive**. The metadecision that precedes a decision is figuring around when to decide fast and when to decide slow.

6. **People need to grasp that we're all in the same boat and connected, and each one is responsible for what happens.** People who acknowledge their connectedness to others will be faster to grasp the big picture and find good solutions than those who don't.

7. **The arrow of time only goes in one direction, at least for us humans.** If you try to go backward

or dig into past decisions, it can create significant legal problems (and other issues). Try to keep moving forward. This also reinforces the idea that before you pull the trigger, you need to consider carefully and do some due diligence, because after that you basically have to "fire and forget."

8. **Understand that no one knows everything, but there are some things that you (or your staff) will be expected to know.** If you (or your staff) don't know something, it is not embarrassing to admit that, because no one knows everything, except when it pertains to basic, routine, ordinary course, core functions of the business that you purport to be in. That means not that you feign knowledge where it doesn't exist but that you make sure you educate yourself and train your staff in the basics before you expose yourself (or them) to the public.

Fifteen Guidelines on MV Accident Risk

This may seem like humor, but your employees have value, and it would be a shame to lose any of them in a senseless motor-vehicle (MV)–related mishap. So here's some risk management advice, derived from real-life incidents:

1. Follow the law—for example, a full stop at a red light or stop sign at a corner before turning into oncoming traffic would prevent many accidents.
2. Speed is usually a factor in accidents, as is substance abuse or intoxication.

3. When driving into a restaurant parking lot, observe the arrow sign so you don't go in the wrong way. And don't drive the wrong way down a street just to do a shortcut into a driveway (I have actually seen someone do this).

4. If turning left to get into the opposing lane is a problem or if turning left across the opposing lane to get into a driveway is a problem, then consider going around the block and avoiding the risks associated with crossing against the traffic or with holding up cars behind you while you wait.

5. Speeding up and slowing down while you are driving can violate the expectations of those around you. This is often a factor when you are changing lanes or someone else is changing lanes. Hesitation and indecision can also increase the likelihood of an accident because you are not clearly signaling your intentions to other drivers.

6. Don't jaywalk, skateboard, or ride a bike at night on a road while wearing very dark clothes because by the time someone who is speeding sees you, it may be too late. Similarly, it might not be a good idea to sit on a curb of a busy street, particularly at night, while wearing black and staring into your smartphone (I actually saw a guy doing this). If you are driving at night, make sure that your headlights are on. The problem isn't that you can't see the road; the problem is that others can't see you, particularly if your car is painted a dark color.

7. If you are walking on a sidewalk by a road and you drop something on the road, don't step off

the sidewalk onto the road to pick it up unless you first check to see that you are not being approached by a car. More generally, don't walk on a street designed for cars.

8. If you are digging around in your parked car on the street with the car door open and your rear end is sticking out into the road, remember that your arse doesn't have eyes and cannot see an approaching car.

9. If you are walking across a driveway or in a parking lot or a crosswalk, don't have your face buried in your smartphone. Look in the direction in which you're going. And consider looking around now and then because danger doesn't always come from in front of you.

10. If you are walking on the sidewalk or even a promenade, don't weave back and forth because a bicycle coming from behind fast may not expect that movement. Some people have been killed by bicyclists on the sidewalk because of the sheer speed at which a bicycle is moving.

11. If you are waiting to parallel park and the driver of the car in the space you want to go into is trying to enter traffic, be aware that you may be blocking the driver's line of sight to the oncoming traffic. This can also be an issue for a driveway that is near the car that is pulling out.

12. If you are changing lanes or entering a driveway, make sure you have enough room in front of you so that you don't get stuck with the rear end of

your car extending out into traffic and blocking the movement of other cars.

13. When backing up in your vehicle, check first to see that the area is clear—and I don't mean just looking in the rearview mirror. I will often open the door and get out of the car to make sure that I have complete clearance.

14. When you approach a driveway or intersection, scan for pedestrians. And recognize please that if you are in the right lane at an intersection getting ready to turn right, the first contact with pedestrians will likely come from your right, not your left, so you should be first scanning to the right—that is, look where you're going.

15. Attitude matters. Don't let the drivers of other cars pressure you. They may be angry, but you don't want to get flustered. And if there is activity around you, such as another car is parking in a nearby stall, be patient and wait for the activity to end before you initiate your moves.

Twelve Nuggets of Wisdom

1. The Bible—Micah 6:8— "He hath showed thee, O man, what is good; and what doth the Lord require of thee, but to do justly, and to love mercy, and to walk humbly with thy God?"

2. Rudyard Kipling—*If*—"If you can talk with crowds and keep your virtue, or walk with kings, nor lose the common touch."

3. Benjamin Franklin—"If your head is wax, don't walk in the sun."

4. Abraham Maslow—"When you're a hammer, everything looks like a nail."

5. Albert Einstein—"A solution should be as simple as possible, but no simpler."

6. Shakespeare—*Hamlet*—"There are more things in heaven and earth, Horatio, than are dreamt of in your philosophy."

7. St. Francis de Sales—"Never be in a hurry; do everything quietly and in a calm spirit. Do not lose your inner peace for anything whatsoever, even if your whole world seems upset."

8. Voltaire—"What is tolerance? It is the consequence of humanity. We are all formed of frailty and error; let us pardon reciprocally each other's folly. That is the first law of nature."

9. Susan Phillips—"But we live day to day, and all those little, seemingly unimportant things are what add up to making our lives."

10. Winston Churchill—"Nourish your hopes, but do not overlook realities."

11. W. A. Mozart—"All I insist upon is that you show the world that you're not afraid."

12. Lewis Carroll—"Life, what is it but a dream?"

About the Author

The author has worked in government and business as a manager and a lawyer. For over a decade, he oversaw a small family business founded by his parents. He also has long experience in business law and finance and has helped to implement a number of government interventions in the market. He has a BA in English literature from Columbia University, a JD from UCLA, a MBA from the University of Hawaii at Manoa, and the CPCU designation. He has written four books: Reinventing Government: A Practitioner's Guide, Basic Stuff That Everyone Should Know, Beyond Obamacare: Solving the Healthcare Cost Problem, and No More Stupidtry: Insights for the Modern World. He uses his trademark "Lloyd Lim Solutions" for pro bono and consulting initiatives. His long term strategic goal is to foster economic improvement through education, rightsizing government, business development and reduction of unnecessary friction. He lives in Honolulu, Hawaii, and enjoys playing the piano.